How Prayer

Helps Me

How Prayer

Helps Me

Edited by
SAMUEL DUFF McCOY

The Dial Press · New York

Printed in the United States of America

Contents

The Contributors

v

To the Reader

HERE ARE the voices of men and women whose faith that their lives are guided by the Unseen God is as simple and complete as that of a child who puts his hand in his father's hand as they set out upon an errand together. Here, too, are the voices of men and women who earnestly pray to the same Unseen God—although they may not always call it prayer— to guide and help them in their daily strivings. Such aspiration is seen crystal clear, in the work of their hands and brains; it is clear to all the world, in their daily lives; and all the world, even the unbelieving world, knows in its secret heart that it is counted among those who thirst for "still waters" of peace; who, each day, rejoice in the beautiful world spread out before all peoples; whose often downcast spirits are comforted by a Certainty; who, undiscouraged by the fact that five thousand years of recorded history have shown barely discernible progress, if any, in human conduct, *know* that a day will dawn whose light will never darken into night.

Here are the voices of men and women of courage:

courage joined to perseverance in their various paths; paths of public and private service, in the arts, in science, commerce, industry, education, and, most of all, in the home.

In their lives, these men and women exemplify the deepest foundations of the American Commonwealth —the insistence upon freedom from autocratic rule; upon freedom of religious belief; upon freedom from intolerance toward others; upon freedom of opportunity; and upon equality before the law. Not one of them insists that all other men pray only as he does.

Nor was any asked to do so.

Each was asked to say, of his own free will, in what manner prayer had benefited himself alone—a request so deeply personal that a compliance could scarcely be hoped for.

But the answering voices are here.

Each witness here has *testified*—upon an oath required by a court higher than any earthly court, the court of his own conscience; yes before the altar of that little church without walls, the invisible Little Church of Those Who Stumble but Keep On—as to what he himself knows. No one on earth can challenge that testimony.

Some of those who were invited to speak, burdened as they were with private or public responsibilities of great weight, could not find the time for reply. From them, and from you who read this, whoever you may be, a message will be welcomed; and, if opportunity offers, it will be passed along to others.

When it is too dark to see one's own path, it is comforting to hear another voice, an understanding voice; and thus to know that you are not alone.

SAMUEL DUFF MCCOY

Glen Cove, Long Island
January, 1955

Prayer

No one ever won complete victory over his temptations or obtained satisfying light on his religious perplexities apart from the practice of looking to God in prayer.

God is our Heavenly Father; and prayer is simply talking with Him.

Even if a man does not believe in prayer he should pray—for the simple reason that prayer is one thing which can be verified only by praying. . . .

The harder it is for a man to pray, the more he needs to pray.

Wherever possible, we should get alone at least once each day for solitary prayer.

If there is no room to which we can retire for this purpose, we might pray as we walk along at night under the open heavens, or in some secluded place during the day.

This suggests the value and necessity of acquiring the habit of looking to God many, many times during the day, wherever we are and in whatever circumstances. If a man is tempted at four o'clock he should not wait until just before he lies down to sleep before he calls upon God for a help greater than his own.

JOHN R. MOTT, *who has been called "the greatest Christian statesman of his time," received, from Cornell, his first academic degree in 1888. In the following sixty years he circumnavigated the globe not less than four times, together with making unceasing shorter journeys, visiting eighty-three foreign nations and governments in behalf of the work of the International Young Men's Christian Association. France, Siam, Portugal, Italy, Hungary, Greece, Poland, Japan, Czechoslovakia, China, Estonia, Sweden, Finland, and his native land bestowed upon him their highest decorations. On December 10, 1946, Norway's Parliament awarded to Dr. Mott the Nobel Peace Prize. He died at his home in Orlando, Florida on January 31, 1955.*

How Prayer
Helps Me

DEAN ACHESON

Our Strength Is in God

WE HAVE great reserves of spiritual strength from which to draw courage for the tasks ahead. The familiar words of Paul can be a stirring inspiration:

"Wherefore," said Paul, "take unto you the whole armor of God, that ye may be able to stand in the evil day, and having done all, to stand. Stand, there-fore, having your loins girt about with truth, and having on the breastplate of righteousness. And your feet shod with the preparation of the gospel of peace. Above all, taking the shield of faith wherewith ye shall be able to quench all the fiery darts of the wicked." In these ancient words of truth and in-spiration, we find the "wholeness" we seek.

The shield of our faith is inscribed with the Brother-hood of Man, and, with the help of God, we shall direct our endeavors to this end.

DEAN ACHESON *former Secretary of State, United States of America, speaks here, surely, for every citi-zen of the United States.*

The Mainspring of Life

P RAYER to God has been the mainspring of my life. Whatever my influence or success in this world may have been, or is today, I can sincerely and reverently say that it has all been the result of faith and prayer. Both the physical and spiritual functions of prayer are needed to guide us confidently through a maze of doubt and fear, and present us daily before our human kind radiant and full of courage. Prayer has helped me when all other aids and agencies proved futile and without hope. Our entire being is stimulated and inspired by prayer. This is because we are each endowed with the immortal elements of the Infinite Mind.

GEORGE MATTHEW ADAMS, *founder of a service which for forty years has distributed featured news articles throughout the world, has presented notable collections of books and etchings to the National Gallery of Art, Washington, D. C.; and the libraries of Yale University, Tuskegee Institute and Dartmouth College.*

IRVING GLADSTONE BANGHART

Courage: A Prayer

IN THE SILENT scrutinies of self, one is apt to be often haunted by a certain feeling akin to fear,—fear of failure. And this fear of failure must be greatest in reasoning out the problem of Courage. Failure to act quickly and wisely at the first hint of duty constitutes the saddest event in the life of an individual. I refer to an individual desiring to fulfill the highest impulses of a spirited nature. What avail the myriad teachings of the ancient creeds,—the muttering of litanies,—the counting of beads innumerable,—the inspiring songs,—the poems of sublimity,—the Fife and Drum,—when the test of Courage ends in failure?

Ultimate conviction must surely exalt Courage above all pious practice. And this Courage will be of the noblest quality, pure and lofty, serene, composed of self-sacrifice, kindness and honesty. For this impulse of life let all the nations, and each troubled soul, strive. It should be their only prayer.

When arrives the moment that is to test the value of the lessons I have learned, the worth of the principles pointing to life's highest duty, which is Courage, let my actions be consistent with those ideals I profess to reverence. Deign Thou, out of Thy kindly beneficence, O gracious Heavens, to grant this, my single request. And let only the sweet approval of conscience be my reward.

IRVING GLADSTONE BANGHART, *born in Illinois in 1881, studied at Princeton University. Later, relinquishing his occupation as editor and publisher of a newspaper in whose pages he fought for clean local government and neighborly kindlinesses, in his middle years, he returned to a boyhood love—the beautiful arts of the printer and the bookbinder. Since his release from a time-clock, he has traveled the length and breadth of America, saluting the memory of Americans whose idealism was linked with courage.*

Tranquil Evening

I HAVE often and often felt that there was something about genuine joy in things that transcended the person who partook in it; that it was parallel to the Catholic belief in the treasures of merit accumulated by the saints on which less well-endowed Christians could draw in their need. Perhaps I am too complacent in hoping that a life like mine has somehow contributed—not so much through what I spoke or published, but in some mystic way—to the capacity for joy of the rest of mankind.

It is easy now to live in ecstasy. I dare confess that at times I feel as if I understood the ecstasy of Saint Francis . . . or, better still, that of the Christ, white-robed and manly, radiant in the joy of sun and sky and earth that he is at one with . . .

All ambition spent . . . I can appreciate any and every gift to the point of worship and I discover in most creative things done nowadays far more to admire and to enjoy than ever before. I only wish I had the will to passivity becoming to my age.

At times I feel like many a one in the years of

7

Hitler's power who always had a bag ready, in case the Gestapo or its local jackals came to carry him off. I am packed and, with Landor, "ready to depart," but not peppering to do so.

BERNARD BERENSON, *regarded by many as the world's most distinguished writer on the art of the Italian Renaissance, was born in Massachusetts in 1864, but has spent most of his life in Italy. Ernest Hemingway, upon being notified that he was to receive the Nobel Prize in literature in 1954, remarked that the prize should earlier have been awarded to Carl Sandburg and to Bernard Berenson, and to the latter in particular for the lucidity of his prose.*

LOUIS BOUCHÉ

Prayer Is Dynamic

Prayer to God is not primarily purposed for value to oneself, so that I find your question somewhat strongly phrased.

Before I became a practicing Catholic, I used to pray only when in trouble, but it did occur to me that this was a greedy way to behave. Why not also pray when everything seemed rosy, and give thanks to God?

Today prayer means to me humility before the great majesty of our Creator, a sense of mystery and awe which is enriching. The reward of a feeling of communication with God is a tremendous one. This can come to me by forgetting my own interests and offering prayers of praise and thanksgiving. I feel that my petitions should only then be presented. (Even on this earth one usually gets into communication and greets warmly a human friend and benefactor from whom one asks a further favor.)

Many of my petitions have been answered, and if some are not, I accept the fact that it is God's will and that He has His reasons.

I feel that prayer is dynamic, capable of growth and of taking many forms. For example, everything I do all day long, if done as well as I can, can be offered as a prayer of praise to God. How happy my life would be, how unimportant small irritations would become if I could always remember that each thought in itself can be a prayer of submission, of praise, or of thanks.

LOUIS BOUCHÉ, *artist, noted for his mural paintings in the public buildings of Washington, the nation's capitol, and in other cities, strikingly exemplifies in his art the rewards of the idealist and the artist's unflagging devotion in the praise of humanity's noblest strivings.*

OMAR BRADLEY

A Prayer for Peace

I AM ENGAGED in the full-time task, at a time when some men would think in terms of retirement, of contributing what I can to National Defense.

Our research laboratories are working under my guidance on forty-five secret weapons, on the premise that military training can expedite such production, and that experience in waging war confers judgment as to what is most vitally needed toward our war potential.

The greatest weapon against attack always was, and always will be, preparedness. However, our preparedness is often adversely interpreted as preparedness for war, rather than as a justifiable measure for adequate defense. Our enemies point out our preoccupation with the implements and accoutrements of war as militarism.

I think that I speak for the American people when I assert that preparedness is our most potent plea for peace. Weakness invites attack. Strength opposes it. The bully does not challenge an adversary whose shoulders are as broad as his own, and America's military might must today shoulder both her own security and that of the free world. Leadership has been thrust upon us and cannot be evaded.

Our nation's power lies beyond any question in preparedness, but preparedness applies as much to the minds and hearts of men as to the weapons at their command.

The sincere desire for peace which dominates our nation's thinking today is at once an unspoken and never-ending prayer. Prayer is not so much petition as repetition. We are admonished to pray without ceasing.

Thus true prayer is reiterating in every act of our lives our belief in an ideal and its attainment. We must dedicate ourselves to this tireless affirming and reaffirming of our faith and hopes for peace.

Prayer is not beating down divine opposition with a bombardment of words, but the silent and steadfast conviction that a Higher Being disposes of man's destiny and will decide the final outcome in the clash between this world's good and evil.

Prayer for peace is the tenacious expectation of peace, steadfast in our resolve to believe and receive. *Petition and repetition.* When we first fortify our faith, our very preparedness becomes a prayer.

GENERAL OMAR BRADLEY *has served in the United States Army since his graduation from West Point in 1915. In World War II he was Commanding General of the 2nd Corps in their Northern Tunisian and Sicilian Campaigns of 1943, and of the First U. S. Army in the Normandy campaign of 1944. In 1944 he was made Administrator of Veterans' Affairs; in 1946, Chief of Staff, U. S. Army; and from 1949-53, Chairman of the United States Joint Chiefs of Staff. In 1950 he was made General of the Army, a title held by only ten others since the nation was founded. Since 1953, he has been chairman of the board of the Bulova Research Laboratories. He is the United States Representative to the standing group and military commission of the North Atlantic Treaty Organization.*

Without Prayer, No Man Has Strength

THESE are turbulent days. They are days of uncertainty and of difficult decision. They are days, in a certain sense, of the wrath of God, Who seems disposed to release man into his own custody, and abandon him to the devices of his own making.

This would be a terrible fate. It is perhaps the most fearsome to which human nature can be given over. Because man without God is man without any measure by which to live.

Those of us who devote our lives to the maintaining of that modern Holy Grail, the Moral Law, are every day being made increasingly aware of the desperate decline in spiritual standards in our beloved country. It is like a great shadow of sickness across the nation, and can only be the result of neglect of prayer, and gradual disassociation with the Creator of Heaven and earth.

Prayer may not make our problems vanish, or even conveniently solve themselves. But it certainly will serve to put man back into proper proportion with his Maker, and thus rekindle the sense of decency and respect for morality which we stand in danger of for-feiting. Only then will our great nation, under God, continue to flourish, for generations yet to come.

JOSEPH I. BREEN, *who has been in charge of RKO Studios, Hollywood, California, as general manager since 1941, is Director of the Production Code Administration, an organization of all motion-picture producing companies dedicated by the industry to the upholding of high ethical standards. Mr. Breen is also vice-president of the Motion Picture Association of America.*

C. E. BREHM

The Power of Prayer

I NEVER ASK God for anything for myself except wisdom, knowledge, understanding, strength and courage to measure up to the responsibilities in my job, that I may be most helpful to others. My prayers are always for others. It has been my experience that all prayers of mine are answered in one way or another, directly or indirectly. It has been my experience, also, that prayers which are in the interest of others are always answered, and God gives us the other material things that we need without asking for them; and a peace and contentment of mind that is worth far more than money or material things. This has been the case in my life, and He has given me far more in material things than I need, or deserve.

God is an inexhaustible source of power for everyone who through prayer calls upon Him for it. I have experienced this many, many times. It will carry one through trying ordeals—problems and situations that one could not otherwise meet. And like the leper out of the ten that were healed by the Christ, I never fail to thank God for answering my prayers. The most satisfying thing to me in life is that God has never failed me, in spite of the fact I have been a disappointment to Him many times.

I can reflect on ordeals that only that great power of God could bring me through. It is unfortunate that so many people are not aware of this great power of God, which is available to all if they will only call upon Him for it.

The greatest need of the world today is prayer and the practicing of God's way of life. When we analyze the problems of the world today we see that they are caused by thinking of self first. God's way of life is for people to think of the welfare of others, be helpful and so live from day to day. Prayer will develop this attitude of mind on the part of an individual. It is the only way people can live harmoniously with each other, and at the same time get the greatest contentment from life.

The greatest legacy my parents ever gave me was taking me to Sunday School and Church and bringing me up to know God, His infinite love, mercy and power, and conversations with Him through prayer. It has meant more to me than anything in my life.

Dr. C. E. Brehm *is president of the University of Tennessee, at Knoxville, Tennessee.*

These Three Things I Would Ask

I'M AFRAID I'm not much of a churchman, and I don't pray; but I try to live a decent life, and be fair in my dealings.

If I did pray, I would ask for peace; and for an end of intolerance; I would ask for better security for the masses; and for an end of greed for power, that seems to cause most of the crises in this unsettled world.

Perhaps, in thinking this, I *have* been praying.

ARTHUR WILLIAM BROWN, *a notable figure for an entire half-century in the field of magazine art, having entered that field in 1903, is a past president of the National Society of Illustrators, heading that organization in 1946 and 1947. His drawings have appeared in virtually every important magazine in this country, illustrating stories by O. Henry, Booth Tarkington, Arthur Train, and other writers. At seventy-four, he is creatively at work in his New York studio.*

The Faith of an Artist

IT IS NOT given to all of us to have a dramatic answer to prayer, such as was accorded to Captain Eddie Rickenbacker, whose miraculous rescue is so well-known. I never had such, but then, I have never been in such a desperate situation either. In less obvious and spectacular ways I have had prayers answered and have found the use of prayer a source of deep spiritual satisfaction.

In I Thessalonians, Chapter 5, Verse 17, we are admonished by St. Paul to "pray without ceasing." This, I take it, is not so much an invitation to indulge in prayer marathons, as it is to be always, no matter where we are, or what we are doing, in a prayerful mood: that is, in readiness of spirit to acknowledge to our God our obligations, our shortcomings, and appreciation of and thankfulness for Divine blessings. Perhaps on a walk or a sketching trip, the beauty of the natural world, or some aspect of weather suddenly seems almost too great to be borne—a prayer of thankfulness leaps almost unbidden from the heart, and seems to ease the pain of beauty. Again it may

19

be the escape from a potentially dangerous situation. Recently I was driving on a narrow country road; coming up to a blind grade, without thinking, I not only, as was proper, pulled over to the right side of the road but, (contrary to my custom), onto the shoulder as fast as I could. At the top of the rise, I met a truck which was far over on the wrong side of the road. Had I been where I had a right to be we would have collided; as it was, since I was so far off the road, the driver of the truck was able to pull away in time. Not to have thanked God for my escape then, or to have attributed it to "luck" would have been ungrateful indeed.

There are so many occasions throughout the day which call for prayer of one kind or another. At meal time, a petition at the beginning for the blessing of and presence of our Lord, and at the end, thankfulness for sustenance, not only is right and proper, but also adds grace and dignity to what might otherwise be a purely physical experience.

Our Saviour himself has given us explicit directions on how to pray. In John, Chapter 15, Verse 16, He says ". . . that whatsoever ye shall ask of the Father in my name, He may give it you." "In my name"—there is nothing ambiguous about that phrase. And always with the qualification which He Himself added: "not my will, but Thine be done." If we in our ignorance ask for something that is not good for us it will naturally be withheld by our all-wise Father, whose only concern is for our welfare, temporal and eternal. Many years ago, the summer after I had graduated from high school, I was taken ill with typhoid fever. Inasmuch as I had planned to go to art school in September, and room with my high school chum, the disappointment seemed unreasonable and too great to bear. And indeed many years were to pass before I realized that it was that last year at home, when my roots went so much deeper into my family life and my environment, that gave the real flavor to my whole subsequent career. God did not need to appear in a vision and say "wait a year," but used the illness as a restraint.

Jesus has also given us that most perfect and comprehensive of all prayers, the one universally known as the Lord's Prayer. Drab and materialistic indeed would each day seem to be to us if we did not at least once repeat it over, not perfunctorily or hastily, but slowly with careful consideration of each petition.

Perhaps someone has done me a wrong—no matter what his subsequent action may be, restitution or otherwise—the incident cannot possibly be closed satisfactorily unless I have first asked God for the

21

grace to forgive him; a prayer that comes easier if I reflect that no one can possibly do one-tenth to me of what I myself have done to both man and God.

The most frequently needed prayer of all is of course the one for forgiveness of my own sins. The knowledge that, if asked for in true repentance, and relying only on the atonement of Christ, full forgiveness will be granted, is the deepest satisfaction to be had, and indeed all that makes life, or living with one's self endurable.

In my own field, the one bogey of every creative artist is the fear that sometime his creative powers will run out; that he will be "through"; and each time an ever-recurring sterile period comes upon him, he thinks this is "it." Sad to say, in this situation I may struggle for days trying to take up my painting again, and it is only then in desperation that I pray God for help. Almost invariably the next day the spell is broken, I awake full of eagerness to work, and ideas begin to flow. There is nothing odd about this— where did the talent come from in the first place?

So all-embracing is this power of petition that God sometimes has the answer to a prayer all ready before the need is apparent to us. In Isaiah, Chapter 65, Verse 24, He says "and it shall come to pass that *before* they call, I will answer." Recently, our son who was in the service in the Far East contracted a disease which eventually forced his return to this country. Some time later, the war in Korea broke out; at that time our prayer certainly would have been that if it was in accordance with His will our son would be spared that ordeal. But the prayer was already answered before we had "called" and the only prayer needed was one of gratitude.

If all this tends to give the appearance of unbearable smugness perhaps I can lessen such an impression by confessing that the foregoing represents more the ideal rather than the actual observance. Like so many of us I do not make the full use of prayer that I should. I do not praise on every occasion I should, or express gratitude or ask forgiveness. But there is no harm in having a high ideal to aim at, always to keep trying as Saint Paul advises, to "pray without ceasing."

CHARLES E. BURCHFIELD, *member of the National Institute of Arts and Letters, has pursued his career as an artist during the past thirty years with distinguished success. His paintings have been acquired by leading museums of art in this country.*

The Sure Reward

IN MY experience, there is great reward in prayer. There is the inward reward you get when you pray alone; and there is the outward reward that comes when many people pray together for a common good and common strength. The latter is like the singing together of Luther's hymn, "Our Lord a Mighty Fortress Is."

I do not know why this is so, nor do I much care. I only know it is. It is a mystery, but those who deny the mystery, never having experienced it, seem to me like men who having brown eyes themselves, deny that other men may have blue eyes. And too often these brown-eyed men, having prayed for something definite, deny the mystery because the definite thing for which they prayed did not happen.

That seems to me a common mistake; almost a universal one. If it helps a man, or men, gives them courage and hope to pray for something definite, that is good; the error comes in expecting an answer as definite as the thing asked. That would be the translating of the particular into the terms of the universal. No man with his finite mind can possibly tell what his individual request will resemble transmuted into the universal need; the ageless process of change.

The only question of importance, it seems to me, is whether prayer does the individual good; and so, if all individuals prayed, would do humanity good. To that question, it seems to me, experience has answered an overwhelming assent.

Man is a lonely creature, shut off from actual contact with his kind, even the nearest and dearest. To keep his place in this world he must assume at times a certain arrogance, but he is actually humble and fearful. There is no way to pierce the veil between himself and his kind, between himself and nature, between himself and what lies back of everything, except to kneel down and forget himself in humbleness and receptivity. It doesn't make much difference how he prays or what he says: it is the act and the relinquishment of self that count.

If man will do this, he will find himself refreshed and closer to the universal, if only for a little while. But if he does it enough, moments added to moments make hours.

STRUTHERS BURT, *distinguished novelist, a member of the National Institute of Arts and Letters, died August 27, 1954.*

Look Up to God for Guidance

I AM GLAD to testify to my faith in prayer to God as a major source of strength and guidance. Prayer from the heart tunes in with the Infinite. Whoever seeks to see and do the will of God on earth shares the mission of the Infinite and will do his task the better for it. Whoever makes the Lord's prayer his prayer and its performance his daily mission will learn much of the Fatherhood of God, the Brotherhood of Man, the wisdom of the Infinite, and will be the better for it.

HAROLD H. BURTON, *Associate Justice of the Supreme Court, born in Jamaica Plain, Massachusetts, June 22, 1888, was graduated from the Harvard Law School in 1912 and began the practice of law in that same year, in Cleveland, Ohio. He served in the United States Army from 1917 to 1919, and was awarded the Croix de Guerre by Belgium. In 1935, after having served as acting Mayor of Cleveland, he was elected Mayor and served until 1940, when he was elected United States Senator. On October 1, 1945, he was appointed to the Supreme Court by President Truman.*

JOHN ALDEN CARPENTER

For the Help That I Constantly Need

YOUR QUESTION has stirred me deeply. You ask me if I have found any inward reward from prayer in my own experience. I can answer strongly in the affirmative, as you can see from a very recent experience in my own life. Two years ago in New York, where I was attending a first performance of one of my new compositions, I suffered a severe fall which resulted in a broken hip. I was taken in hand by a remarkable bone surgeon at the hospital in New York, and from that moment on I have found that the difficulties of my personal situation could only be improved by learning how to pray; and from that moment on I have been constantly aided by developing my own ability to pray for the help that I need— for difficulties resulting not only from my physical weakness but for my own musical aspirations, which I was trying to keep alive all through this critical period.

JOHN ALDEN CARPENTER, *one of America's finest composers of music—winner of the Gold Medal of* the National Institute of Arts and Letters in 1947, and of other honors—wrote this statement at a time when he had been tortured by physical illness which had continued for two years, not for the few weeks that had at first been expected. This ordeal he daily faced with a fortitude derived from his daily prayers to God. In April, 1951, when "lo, the winter is past, the flowers appear on the earth, the time of the singing of birds is come," John Alden Carpenter, leaving the room in which he had listened to melodies yet unheard, surely went "out of doors" with joy, to hear symphonies beyond those of earth.

ELBERT N. CARVEL

God's Will Be Done, Not Mine

YOU ASK me for what do I pray. I pray that God's will be done, not my will be done; I pray that God will give me the grace and knowledge to understand and to do His will; I pray that God will help me be kind and understanding to my fellowman, that He will help me to do my part to relieve the pain and suffering and distress that constantly besets humanity, that He will help me to make my contribution to the development of a lasting and a just peace.

ELBERT NOSTRAND CARVEL, *industrialist, was elected Governor of Delaware in 1948, serving as Governor from 1949 to 1953. He had been Lieutenant-Governor of the State from 1945 to 1949, and concurrently president of the State Board of Pardons. He resides in Laurel, Delaware.*

Why We Need to Pray

THE RELATIONSHIP of prayer to our spiritual and temporal welfare is a challenging subject for speculation.

Nothing is taught more clearly in every portion of the Bible than that God desires that we should pray to Him. Not only did the Lord teach mankind the eloquent prayer that bears His name, but Christ's words unmistakably show that he wishes us to pray.

Christ particularly said: "Whatsoever ye shall ask in My name, that will I do." The Epistles of Saint Paul and Saint John contain numerous admonitions to pray.

Prayer is described as the lifting of our hearts and minds to God to adore, praise, and thank Him, and to ask blessings for ourselves and others. It is man's tribute to God, his spiritual Father. But, aside from paying rightful tribute to God, prayer is a powerful weapon for us as individuals.

Prayer is the stalwart sword of the spirit—giving the soul the source to defend itself against the vicissitudes of life; a healing ointment for the wounds

30

suffered in life's battles. Prayer can strengthen us in virtue and draw us closer to God. As a medium of intercession, it can be the means of bringing greater blessings upon ourselves, our children, our homes, our communities, our Nation and the world.

Unfortunately, men forget that prayer is a vital force in their lives. A nation—or a world—is only as strong as its people, its families, its communities. Individually and collectively, these can constitute a bulwark of strength against the forces of evil, if men will but realize, and resort to the power of prayer.

Today, world peace is threatened because many men, forgetting the Divine Savior and that blessedness born of obedience to His Almighty Law, have followed their own selfish desires and excluded Him from their personal lives and from human affairs.

With the world divided into two camps—the forces of anarchy, oppression, class hatred, anti-religion, immorality and disaster on the one side, and the forces of religion, right, order, morality, truth, justice and peace on the other—there is a greater need than ever before to return to righteous thinking and living, and to pray for justice and peace with firm faith and confidence in God.

Where God is deliberately excluded, there can be no unity of purpose, no brotherhood of men, no real freedom, no true peace among men or among nations.

A great deal has been written in our time about the alleged failure of Christianity. It is not Christianity that has failed, but that far too many so-called Christians have not followed the teachings and precepts of Christianity.

The present world situation emphasizes this failure in rather brutal fashion. If the individual and collective influence of Christians in every country had been strong, if many nations and their leaders had not become materialistic in outlook, the crisis the world faces today would not have occurred.

It is one of the grave tragedies of our times that many professed Christians have ceased to pray; they have ceased to look to God as their Father. Thus, they have forgotten that all men are brothers under the Fatherhood of God, entitled to "life, liberty and the pursuit of happiness" in a world free of oppression and tyranny.

In these times the security of the human spirit can be strengthened through full awareness of the meaning of brotherhood among all men, regardless of race or nationality or economic status. We need to pray to God that such awareness will come to all Americans and to all nations.

In the words of the great Saint Francis of Assisi

we may gain strength for our task through this prayer:

"Lord, make me an instrument of Thy peace; where there is hatred, let me sow love; where there is injury, pardon; where there is doubt, faith; where there is despair, hope; where there is darkness, light; where there is sadness, joy. O Divine Master, grant that I may not seek so much to be consoled as to console; to be understood as to understand; to be loved as to love; for it is in giving that we receive, it is in pardoning that we are pardoned, and it is in dying that we are born to eternal life."

OSCAR LITTLETON CHAPMAN, *former Secretary of the Interior, was born in Virginia. He was admitted to the Colorado Bar in 1929 and began the practice of law in Denver. He was appointed Assistant Secretary of the Interior in 1933 and was advanced to Under-Secretary in 1946. In 1949 he became Secretary of the Interior, serving to 1953, completing twenty years in that Department. He continues his private law practice in Washington, D. C.*

Prayer the Source of Character and Strength

PRAYER is an experience of fellowship with the Power that creates and sustains life. It is a source of character and strength equal to whatever demands life may impose.

Prayer deepens our understanding of God's will for our lives. When we pray "Thy kingdom come," we share as far as we are able the divine perspective.

Prayer strengthens our resolve to live in harmony with the purposes of our Creator. When we pray "Thy will be done," we subordinate our own strivings to His ends that are greater than ourselves. Prayer renews our commitment to a society of good will and brotherhood among men.

Prayer quickens our faith. An experience of prayer confirms the reality of the spirit of God in our lives.

Prayer is power. When the will and mind of man are in harmony with the creative Spirit that undergirds the universe, man has new resources for effective living. He, too, shares in the ongoing creative process by realizing spiritual values in his own life and his community.

In these miraculous ways prayer constantly changes the quality and the course of our lives.

TOM C. CLARK, *Associate Justice of the Supreme Court of the United States, served as Attorney-General of the United States prior to his appointment to the Supreme Court.*

35

There Is No Happy Life without Prayer

I T IS MY firm conviction that a man cannot lead a happy life without the spiritual uplift which comes through communion with God by means of daily prayer; it is as important, I believe, as our heart-beats. The only attachment we have to the eternal is by means of prayer to God, the ruler of the universe —omnipotent, unseen, but, nevertheless, ever present. The spirit of God is present in everyone and I believe that spirit may only be awakened and kept alive through prayer. Two thousand years ago the prophet Micah wrote: "He hath shewed thee, O man, what is good; and what doth the Lord require of thee, but to do justly, and to love mercy, and to walk humbly with thy God?" Life can only be rich and full if we call upon the Giver of Life to help us to help others as well as ourselves, and by walking and talking with the God of our Fathers; in my humble opinion, this is an indispensable guide along the pathway to peace.

GILMORE D. CLARKE *was landscape architect of the Westchester County (N. Y.) Park System and sub-*

sequently served as consultant to the Department of Parks, City of New York. He has also served on the National Commission of Fine Arts and as Professor of Regional Planning and Dean of the College of Architecture, Cornell University. He was a member of the Board of Design, New York World's Fair. He is a member of the American Academy of Arts and Letters.

My Closest Companion

Prayer is described by the poet as "The soul's sincere desire, uttered or unexpressed." This is true in part only. It does express an attitude and a conscious dependence upon some higher power beyond self.

To me, prayer is a personal communion with a personal God, who is my Creator and who always seeks to develop in me those attributes which contribute to my highest good.

God abides within my soul, a real personality which we call "the Holy Spirit." My communion with God, my prayer to God is what I say to this Holy Spirit and what I hear in response.

I find prayer to be a simple and natural thing. God is my closest companion, always ready to hear my plea and give immediate help, guidance and counsel. I am always conscious of God's presence and his loving care. He hears my expressions of gratitude as well as my request for counsel and guidance in making decisions.

Prayer is then an attitude of mind, an emotion of

the heart, a companionship of spirit with spirit. *My sin is self-sufficiency*—when I exercise my own judgment and forget to ask God's counsel. Then I often make grievous errors.

When God's Holy Spirit and my spirit tread life's pathway together in loving companionship, there are no mistakes. It is then easy to "trust and obey." Prayer helps me forget the errors of yesterday—live right today and have no worries about tomorrow.

WILLIAM COFFIN COLEMAN, *manufacturer, civic leader, born in Chatham, New York in 1870, entered business in Kansas and founded the Coleman Company, Inc., in Wichita. He served as City Commissioner and later was elected Mayor of Wichita. A leading Baptist layman, he was president of the Northern Baptist Convention.*

Ann Connolly's Prayer

ANN (O'DONNELL) CONNOLLY was born and lived in the island of Aranmore of the Aran Islands off Galway Bay. She was a devout Catholic as were almost all the Aran Islanders, as was her husband Sean Tammas (John Thomas) Connolly. They married young, Ann at seventeen and Sean at twenty-five. Ann was twenty-one years and she had two children, young Sean three years and little Sarah one year, when the great trial came into her life—and Sean's.

Ann's mother, Mary O'Donnell, was a widow with two teen age sons; good sons both, laboring industriously and doing pretty well at making a living for themselves and their widowed mother. It was then a smallpox epidemic swept over the Arans from the mainland and struck down Mary O'Donnell's two young sons.

When Ann Connolly heard of the danger to her two young brothers she hurried over to console her mother, and offer her a home with herself and her Sean if the young boys died—this, when to her and the neighbors it looked as if the two lads could not possibly live. Mary O'Donnell said no to Ann's offer of a home. "No, Ann, I must not be a burden to you, the good daughter you have always been, and to your grand husband, Sean Tammas. I'll make out, have no fear."

But Ann Connolly did have a fear and she so said to Sean Tammas, adding: "The proud one, mother is! I don't know what I'm going to do." Young Ann gave the matter much thought, even to getting down on her knees and praying to God for guidance. While still on her knees the light came to her. She told Sean Tammas, who was home from sea at the time, of her plan to save her brothers and so help her mother. Sean agreed to let her have her way.

There was a holy shrine on Aranmore, Saint Ann's Shrine, and there was her own name, Ann; and now was not the first time she would be praying to Saint Ann for help. There was a heavy fall of snow that week—an extraordinary thing in the Arans. Ann trudged through the deep snow to Saint Ann's Shrine and offered up her prayer; "Dear God, don't let my poor mother's two young sons die! What will become of her if they die, she with no other support, and the good woman she has been? No, dear God, don't. If You must have the two sacrifices let the two lads live and take my two children in their place. Please, dear God, and do you Saint Ann, add your prayers to mine. My Sean and myself are both young and strong, and in nature and the goodness of God we will have more children."

That night Ann Connolly nursed her infant Sarah, lullabied Sarah and young Sean to sleep. They were two healthy children with never a sick day in their lives; but two days later the smallpox took them; and that same day young Jimmie and Johnnie O'Donnell began to get well. They recovered and some years later came to America with their mother and settled in Boston where they lived, Jimmie to eighty-two years of age and Johnnie to one hundred and five—he died a few years ago, his mind clear to the last. Jimmie had an early death for one of his family, being killed when he tried to beat a passenger train to a street crossing. Mary O'Donnell died at eighty-nine.

John and Ann Connolly preceded the O'Donnells to Boston, where Ann Connolly had her hope of more children. They had nine sons and one daughter, eight sons in a row, of which sons I was the fifth; and the nine American-born grew up to a healthy and happy maturity and well beyond, excepting one, two-year-old John who was scalded to death. My mother died at the age of ninety-three.

Fifty odd years after my parents left the Arans for this country I visited there to see the land where my ancestors were born. In Aranmore I met elderly folk who recalled the wedding day of young Ann O'Donnell (Fair Annie) and Sean Connolly. Some of them recalled the deaths of Sean and Ann's two babies; I said a prayer at their grave cover—a wide slate with the names John Connolly and Sarah Connolly, on the slab, the same strewed with sand washed up from the bay (Galway Bay) beach below—and for the recovery from death's door of Mary O'Donnell's two young sons.

JAMES BRENDAN CONNOLLY, *born in Boston in the 1870's, has had all through his life a way of amalgamating prayer and the work of his own hands, brain, and soul. After working as clerk, inspector and surveyor in the U. S. Engineering Corps in Georgia, from 1892-95, and saving enough to attend Harvard, he decided to enter the Olympic Games of 1896 at Athens, Greece, and, working his way across on a freighter, won the first Olympic championship of modern times. He served in the war with Spain in 1898, was at the siege of Santiago, and, ten years later, served in the United States Navy. His first book, Out of Gloucester, was published in 1902; in the fol-*

lowing forty years twenty-four other books were published. In 1902, Mr. Connolly reported for *Harper's Magazine* what he saw on a voyage to the Arctic Ocean; for *Collier's*, in 1914, what he saw of the fighting in Mexico; and, also for *Collier's*, the naval operations in European waters in 1917 and 1918.

A Source of Power and Faith

WORSHIP is the highest of all arts. And certainly today, when millions live in fear and insecurity, we need to turn to prayer as a source of power and faith. We are so accustomed to being restless and busy that it will seem rather difficult at first to stop long enough for regular devotional periods. Yet only through prayer can we enjoy spiritual communion with the divine.

The first thing our forefathers did when they got off the ship was to kneel down and thank God. Each man was seeking His presence, reading His Word, listening to His voice, trying to understand His way and to live by it. Only as we ask God for guidance and direction can we be lifted into the way in which we should go.

DR. GEORGE L. CROSS is President of the University of Oklahoma, at Norman, Oklahoma.

The Belief in Man's Soul

THE DISBELIEF in what we may call the soul has had tremendous consequences. On the one hand there is the reasoning which says that if only the *Here* and the *Now* exist, and all else is a blank, one should get what one can, with no regard for means—that is, we have a return to the law of the jungle. On the other hand, others reason from the same premise that if we give a man enough material things and comforts, he will be happy and content. From one we have the burgeoning of rugged individualism during the nineteenth and early twentieth centuries, the piracy period, which came to an end after World War I. From the other we have the defeatist solution of collectivism in various forms, a device of the qualitative rather than the quantitative mind, a triumph of the wishbone over the backbone. Both solutions are truly reactionary; both tie into the fundamental thesis of the complete efficacy of the satisfaction of material wants, the first for himself alone and the second for a collective self of no different mental attitude. Both are reactionary because they revert to systems worn out in the early history of the human race, and the second leads inevitably to despotism, a collective emperor being perhaps worse than an individual one.

What can we do, and particularly what can we chemists and chemical engineers do, in our particular segment of life to counteract these reactionary tendencies? How can we strike an all-round balance? We can re-create in ourselves the belief in man's soul and its all-importance.

Few universities get beyond stuffing the mind to training the soul. Much is made of the fact that since we cannot agree in matters of religion, it must be eliminated from education. This is straight escapism.

By recognizing that no business can be entirely an individual thing and likewise that its human parts are not machines but souls, industry would solve many problems now being attacked by nonexperimental doctrinaires.

Science has been only a partial success because it early fell into the hands of materialists and hence has had a lopsided development, which has accentuated problems without presenting means for their correction. For these reasons we have had two reactionary movements, on the one hand a return to rugged individualism, the law of the jungle and the first state of man; and on the other hand to authoritarianism in its

47

forms of fascism and collectivism, a reaction to the second state of man, despotism.

Let us therefore throw out the materialistic view of life, concede to the social sciences and religion their equality with the physical, perhaps even their superiority, and help them catch up with us and prevent a further descent into the past. You can depend upon it, no scientist will be hurt as a scientist by having a developed soul.

FRANCIS J. CURTIS *is vice-president of the Monsanto Chemical Company. A graduate of Harvard in 1915, he has served as a consultant to the United States Government and is a vice-president of the American Institute of Chemical Engineers, as well as being a past-chairman of the American section of the International Society of Chemical Industry.*

My Faith

I HAVE a strong personal belief and reliance on the power of prayer for Divine inspiration.

Every person has his own ideas of the act of praying for God's guidance, tolerance and mercy to fulfill his duties and responsibilities. My own concept of prayer is not as a plea for special favors or as a quick palliation for wrongs knowingly committed. A prayer, it seems to me, implies a promise as well as a request.

All prayer, by the humble or the highly placed, has one thing in common, as I see it: a supplication for strength and inspiration to carry on the best human impulses which should bind us all together for a better world. Without such inspiration, we would rapidly deteriorate and finally perish.

WALT DISNEY *was born in Chicago in 1901, and has been producing animated cartoons since 1920. Many of his films have been given awards by the Academy of Motion Picture Arts and Sciences, among them* The Three Little Pigs *in 1933, and* Snow White and the Seven Dwarfs *in 1938.*

GUY PÈNE DU BOIS

To a God of Smiling Companionship

THE NATURE of prayers must depend somewhat upon the nature of the divinity to whom they are addressed. The one I pray to has more in common with the gods of the old Greeks and to that Chinese god, who, in the sculptured renditions of him, always counterbalances the ferocity of his frown with an engaging and sympathetic smile. To this god, who obviously has a sense of humour, one may pray for anything: from luck at a game of solitaire to the hope of finding a check in the morning mail: often quite important to a free-lance artist. To pray for changes on our planet, with which he has been experimenting for millions of years, would seem rather presumptuous.

GUY PÈNE DU BOIS, *artist and critic, whose paintings have been shown in and are owned by many art galleries, in recent years has resided in France. In 1954, a notable collection of his work, including paintings completed in Paris, was exhibited here. He is a member of the National Institute of Arts and Letters. The Altman Prize was awarded him in 1945.*

50

Let Us Pray as Lincoln Prayed

Even though America from the beginning of its settlement has been motivated by religious faith, it is doubtful whether our people ever have had greater need for Divine help and guidance than they do today.

In reaction against the crass materialism which is at the bottom of the disasters that threaten us, the American people increasingly are turning to a belief in prayer to God as the surest means of peace of mind and salvation. They are imploring Divine assistance in the spirit of Abraham Lincoln, who, leaving his home to assume the Presidency at a time when dark and menacing clouds also streaked the American skies, bade farewell to his Springfield, Illinois neighbors in these words:

"A duty devolves upon me which is, perhaps, greater than that which has devolved upon any other man since the days of Washington. He never would have succeeded except by the aid of Divine Providence, upon which he at all times relied. I feel that I cannot succeed without the same Divine aid which sustained him and on the same Almighty Being I place my reliance for support; and I hope you, my friends, will all pray that I may receive that Divine assistance, without which I cannot succeed, but with which success is certain."

ROBERT G. DUNLOP *is President of The Sun Oil Company of Philadelphia, Pennsylvania.*

As Necessary as Breathing

I KNOW that if I let one night slip by without saying my prayers, I wake up the next morning kinda disturbed, thinking how selfish I've been that I did not give a few minutes to prayer.

Prayer and going to church regular gives me a feeling of satisfaction and a feeling inside of me that I can't describe—it's as necessary as breathing.

JAMES FRANCIS DURANTE ("Jimmy" to virtually all the world's peoples and beloved by all who know his courage and his faith), was born in 1893 in New York City and went to work in his father's barber shop as soon as he had attended the public schools for a short while. His first job as a public entertainer began when he was seventeen, as a piano player at Coney Island. Since then he has made life happier (and better) for countless people.

What Prayer Means to Me

PRAYER is as needful in our lives as the air we breathe. No matter what the circumstances, it is a pillar of strength. It helps to solve the problems where education, science, technology and skill fail. It lightens the burden of grief. It becomes the means of expressing to Divine Providence the gratitude of a happy heart.

HARVEY SAMUEL FIRESTONE, JR. *was graduated from Princeton in 1920 and has been actively associated with the Firestone Tire and Rubber Company ever since.*

My Approach to Prayer

A RELIGION of gratitude to God, or a religion of generous hope and of trust in others, is a better one than a religion that assumes one is burdened down with intolerable guilt, and must be saved from that guilt every moment.

We, as human beings, as mammals with a conscience, should enjoy life, should make life worth while every day. By loving mankind, not in selfish but in unselfish ways, we fulfill the human equation.

Our earthly life is symbolized by the bread and wine. Under the appearance of bread and wine God gives himself to us. Thus we are made sharers of His divinity who saw fit to share our humanity.

There is a palpable righteousness in the things that God has made, and that man is God's instrument for making.

JOHN GOULD FLETCHER, *author, born in 1886, to whom the Pulitzer Prize was awarded in 1939 for his*

Selected Poems, *died at his home, "Johnswood," near his birthplace in Little Rock, Arkansas, at the age of sixty-four. His first book,* Fire and Wine, *had been published when he was twenty-seven. In addition to several volumes of poems, he was the author of a biography of Gauguin; a prose history of his native state; translator of works by Elie Faure and Jean Jacques Rousseau, and an account of his own life, published when he was fifty-one, entitled* Life Is My Song. *From the unpublished diaries to which for years he had confided his inmost thoughts, these lines, born of the poet's vision, were selected.*

Look into Our Own Hearts

H ERE in America, we are in the forefront of a new struggle against tyranny. With leadership ours, from the start of time, we face unparalleled military, economic and social responsibilities.

In measuring our ability to meet this challenge, we are relying heavily upon our material resources. But what of our spiritual resources? It seems to me that if we are to provide real leadership, we must be prepared to offer more than military and economic strength. We must offer spiritual strength, too.

Millions of people in other countries are looking to us today for more than guns or bread. They want to believe in us and in our way of life. They want to be assured that freedom and democracy are worth fighting for.

It isn't surprising that others should be confused about America. But I think we should take great care that we ourselves don't get confused about what we stand for and from what we derive our strength.

Some say that we are strong because of our vast natural resources. Others say that the foundation of

American strength lies in our economic system. But neither these nor any other answer in economic terms can explain our basic vitality.

The well-springs of our vitality are not economic. They go far deeper: they are ethical and spiritual.

We believe in man. We believe in men not merely as production units, but as the children of God. We must look for answers within our own hearts. If we are to provide the free-world leadership which is needed right now, it is important—desperately important—that we be very clear in our own minds about the sources of our strength. It is important that we nourish and safeguard the ethical principles which make us strong.

BENSON FORD, *business executive, son of Edsel Ford and grandson of Henry Ford, is a director of the Ford Motor Company and its subsidiaries. He is a member and trustee of the Ford Foundation and Protestant Co-chairman of the National Conference of Christians and Jews. In World War II he served as a captain in the Air Force.*

CLARENCE FRANCIS

We Need Faith

Sᴘᴇᴀᴋɪɴɢ personally, I do not know a single busi-
nessman of any consequence today who would
engage in some of the trade practices and labor poli-
cies that were a comparative commonplace fifty years
ago. No member of my board of directors would
condone a shady or dishonest policy on the part of
our management. And this is not to confer unsolicited
halos on my associates. I think this attitude is quite
general.

Today, most managements, in fact, operate as
trustees in recognition of the claims of employees,
investors, consumers, and government. The task is to
keep these forces in balance and to see that each gets
a fair share of industry's rewards.

We have seen, then, the general acceptance of a
series of "Thou Shalt Nots." No Moses brought them
down from a mountain-top. It just came to be generally agreed that "Honesty is the best policy."

But, having accepted the "Do Nots," are we not
ready now for an era of positive "Do's?"

The Decalogue, after all, did no more than impose

59

certain necessary restrictions on human conduct. A new era began when the Sermon on the Mount opened mankind's eyes to the possibilities of good will.

I am not ashamed to predict to you that the next age of business leadership will belong to those who count their success in terms of the greatest possible service to the greatest number of people. I say that the human problems of industry are the big problems and that they will not yield to techniques alone—important as these may be.

There must be at bottom a will to make business work in the public interest. And preceding that there must be an agreement on motives. Can anyone forget the miraculous unanimity with which we Americans came together in wartime? We were agreed on the reasons why.

Let us now study our own motives as businessmen. Are our "reasons why" good enough for the future?

Why do we get up in the morning and hurry to work? To hold a job? To make a sale? To finish a blueprint? To balance a set of figures? Those are worthy aims—but they are not sufficient as ends in themselves. We need the courage to be moral. Morality is not an accident. We need to be intolerant of evil. There is a vast difference between tolerance

60

of the man who falls short of perfection and tolerance of evil itself.

The only essential difference between us and the other animals is our power of choice. We can nullify that difference—we can be false to the great upward struggle of man—by not throwing the weight of our own actions on the side of good. We can add positively to the stature of man himself by using our God-given power of choice properly. Moral courage has shaken and changed the world for the better before and will do it again. The trend is in the right direction, with much to be done.

Let us reject cynicism in all its forms and accept the challenge of tomorrow. Within and beyond our borders, it is in the realm of moral principle that the real responsibility of businessmen will be discharged. The test of leadership is its capacity to lead. We have the principles and we know them to be sound. We need the faith and the will to make them work.

CLARENCE FRANCIS, *corporation executive, graduating from Amherst in 1910, began his business career in that year and became president of the General Foods Corporation in 1934. Since 1943, he has been chairman of that corporation's board of directors. He resides in Bronxville, New York.*

Prayer Is Constant Thanks

I HOPE Prayer, like breathing, is the constant thanks I try to give and live for all the blessings in this the most perfect of all beautiful worlds.

LILLIAN GISH *has been appearing in motion pictures since 1914. Among her best-known films are* Birth of a Nation, Way Down East *and* Orphans of the Storm. *On Broadway since 1930, Miss Gish has played in* Uncle Vanya, Camille, Hamlet *and* Life with Father.

JOHN GOLDEN

A *Prayer for the Nations, in Unison*

G OD OF THE Measureless Universe . . . Creator
of Man's Conscience . . . to Thee in this our
fervent prayer for peace, we lift our voices in unison.

We . . . Americans of every faith . . . of every
creed . . . join together pleading for truth, justice and
charity among men. We pray for Thy omnipotent
aid in this hour of imperiled civilization.

That Thou shalt cast out forever from human
thought that flaming intolerance which makes for
war and breeds bloody aggression.

That the advocates of war shall beat their swords
into plowshares and their spears into pruning hooks.

We pray to Thee for the restoration of concord
and amity among all the peoples of the earth.

That all persons recognize the liberty due religion,
and for the renewal of the way of life that is fruitful
of great and good works.

This, O Lord, is our fervent prayer, and this is our
mingled tribute to Thy everlasting mercy. *Amen.*

JOHN GOLDEN, *dean of Broadway producers, composed this prayer for United Nations Day.*

PAUL GREEN

An Immortal Trust

M Y PRAYER—if I could call it that—is a constant and ceaseless yearning for peace and cooperation among men. And it is sustained by a faith that the nature of the universe is a beneficent one and that man must, yea will, at least find a way of living in and of that beneficence. If not, then he will have failed his immortal trust and his prayers with him.

PAUL ELIOT GREEN, *author, playwright, Pulitzer Prize winner for his play,* Abraham's Bosom, *is professor of dramatic art, University of North Carolina.*

LOUIS GRUENBERG

A Prayer of Thankfulness

THE FOLLOWING, my daily prayer for many a
year, has been the greatest source of strength in
conquering fear:

> Lord, O Lord, I thank Thee for the many bless-
> ings given me,
> For eyes to behold the magnificence of sky, ocean,
> field and mountain,
> For ears to hear the extraordinarily wonderful
> sounds called music,
> For the exceedingly rare and mystical inner voice
> called inspiration,
> For the great heart that, alone, understands
> what is called love,
> And for a good day's work.
> Lord, O Lord, I thank Thee for the many bless-
> ings given me,
> And for the many evils Thou hast kept from me
> and mine.

LOUIS GRUENBERG, *distinguished in the field of
music, is a member of the National Institute of Arts
and Letters. He resides in Beverly Hills, California.*

LAURENCE C. HART

Patience . . . Courage . . . Wisdom

IN THIS period of national emergency and world-wide crisis, faith in God and reliance upon prayer for divine guidance will motivate the decisions and actions of many of our nation's leaders. All of us, great and small alike, can perhaps find effective guidance for our day-to-day activities in the words of that simple little prayer:

"O Lord, give me the patience to endure the things I cannot change. Give me the courage to change the things I ought to change. And, above all, give me the wisdom to know the difference."

LAURENCE C. HART *is vice president of the Johns-Manville Corporation of New York.*

Be Not Forgetful of Prayer

NEARLY all of my life I have been interested in the subject of prayer, but have failed to master it. Dostoyevsky said, "Be not forgetful of prayer. Every time you pray, if your prayer is sincere, there will be new feelings and new meanings in it, which will give you fresh courage and you will understand that prayer is an education." I believe that learning to pray is an important process in the growth of a Christian life. In personal tribulation, in the hour of temptation, in the struggle against injustice, in every human crisis, the source of Power is available for us through prayer.

BROOKS HAYS *of Little Rock, Arkansas, represents the Fifth Congressional District of the State of Arkansas in the House of Representatives and is a member of the Banking and Currency Committee.*

Prayer—and Man's Freedom

SINCE that first dawn, when man first stood before his Maker, all men have cherished this tremendous thing, this magnificent thing, that makes man a man—his freedom.

Prayer *is* man, speaking to God. And God alone gives him freedom.

But what is this freedom? What right have we to it? Why are we unhappy unless we are free men?

We know that man has no meaning, no worth, no dignity apart from the image of God in him. It is through each of us, as persons, that all greatness springs. Great art, great music, great accomplishments of a nation, are born in the mind of the person. Greatness shines out, too, from the soul of the mother who cooks and washes and mends for her children, who prays, who teaches her children to pray.

The poorest of men has dignity when he looks up to God. Each man, each woman, is the Person through whom God has chosen to manifest Himself.

To many of the youngsters of this year this may not mean too much; but if they only knew, as we older ones know, it is the basis of everything that free men fight and die for: the privilege to remain free men.

Whenever our sons go off to war we should make them aware of what they are doing in defending their liberty. Whether they know it or not they are going out to defend the image of God in themselves, in their families, in their countrymen, and to preserve it for unborn generations yet to come. To wage war for anything less, for economics or politics, is monstrous. Edmund Burke once said, "the blood of man should never be shed but to redeem the blood of man." Only in such a cause will war ever bring a real, a lasting peace.

Real peace is more than the absence of war. It is a tranquillity of order, it is security, liberty—religious, political and economic freedom. Peace permits men to traverse the high seas without violence; it permits all people to choose the form of government under which they will live; it permits all nations to dwell in safety within their own boundaries; it is the abandonment of force and aggression; it is life with honor, life with the dignity of the Children of God. It is both the implement and the goal of human progress. And because we are Children of God, and hungry and thirsty for that strange freedom and stranger peace

69

known only to those who worship God in spirit and in truth, we must never cease our struggles until they are secure forever.

In this struggle for freedom, at home and abroad, our greatest weapon—both a sword and a shield—will be our love of, and faith in God. To open the hearts and minds of men to this truth will require a mighty river of faith and effort. Each one of us is a drop to swell that river and augment its force. And daily prayer, by each one of us, is mighty. Prayer brings action, fortitude, calm.

"Thy will be done—on earth, as it is in Heaven."

This is my daily prayer.

CONRAD N. HILTON *is president of Hilton Hotels, Inc., operators of various large hotels including the Waldorf-Astoria, New York City. As a layman, his aid in the work of the National Conference of Christians and Jews has been notable.*

Refresh Each Day with Religious Devotion

FOR SIX thousand years, since recorded time, every civilized race has believed in a Supreme Being.

The Sermon on the Mount established the transcendent concept of compassion and good will among men.

Freedom does not come like manna from Heaven; it must be cultivated from rocky soil with infinite patience and great human toil.

Our Founding Fathers did not invent the priceless boon of individual freedom and respect for the dignity of men. That great gift to mankind sprang from the Creator and not from governments.

There rise constantly in my mind the forces which make for progress and those which may corrode away the safeguards of freedom in America. I want to say something about these forces, but I shall endeavor to do so, not in the tones of Jeremiah but in the spirit of Saint Paul. . . . A nation is strong or weak, it thrives or perishes upon what it believes to be true. . . . God has blessed us with another wonderful word—heritage. The great documents of that heritage are the

Bible, the Declaration of Independence, and the Constitution of the United States. Within them alone can the safeguards of freedom survive.

Eighty years is a long time for a man to live. As the shadows lengthen over my years, my confidence, my hopes and dreams for my countrymen are undimmed. This confidence is that with advancing knowledge, toil will grow less exacting; that fear, hatred, pain, and tears may subside; that the regenerating sun of creative ability and religious devotion will refresh each morning the strength and progress of my country.

HERBERT HOOVER, *thirty-first President of the United States, was born in West Branch, Iowa, August 10, 1874. He was elected President in 1928, and was renominated in 1932.*

Union with the Power by Which We Live

PRAYER to me is union with the power by which we live.

I pray the Lord's Prayer as the basis of all other praying. I read and meditate on the Psalms, and find their spirit, attitude and music setting the tone of all other praying. I pray privately and in my family from The Book of Common Prayer and find in these prayers wonderful phrasing of my inmost desires and a lift from the narrow circle of my own prayers and meditations. I read such periodical manuals as *Forward* and *The Upper Room,* and recently I have found great strength in the *Meditations* of Kagawa. I read with some constancy *The Imitation of Christ,* and the *Confessions* of Saint Augustine. I pray with the minister in church and with all who offer prayer as from a group. And in addition I pray privately, sometimes articulately and sometimes as a mere aspiration, about anything in my mind and in my business or pleasure.

I pray for personal union with God along the line of firm faith, lively hope, unselfish love, clear thought, and integrated action. I pray for each person in himself, in his family and neighborhood, in work and play, in his institutions, in his state, nation, in the United Nations, in the world whether it be for friend or foe. I pray for all from individual and intimately personal values to as deep and broad concerns as I can possibly imagine, and beyond that I pray that I may know how to pray.

This is all so much a part of my life that I am no more able to assess it than I am to assess food, air, water, love, truth, goodness, beauty. All I can testify is that I would not dare to begin a day, begin a night, or live a moment without providing that my every thought, act, and even sentiment be in God's sight. I do not believe it is up to me to make any assessment, but simply to obey the injunction of Our Lord and His Apostles to pray without ceasing.

Dr. Robert Burton House *is chancellor of the University of North Carolina in Chapel Hill, North Carolina.*

CECIL HOWARD

The Inner Happiness

I T WAS only late in life that I was brought to the conviction of the necessity for daily prayer. The heavy burden which finally led me to seek this help would certainly have been unbearable without the strength given during the last few years in answer to the prayers of my wife and myself.

How much better it would have been had I realized sooner that "man cannot live by bread alone." As long as his "luck" holds one may think he can do without God. Just what is "luck?" And how ungrateful can one be for it until it leaves us?

I have had what is generally called a happy life. Yet through these years of my wife's grave and ago-nizing affliction we have both felt the growth of a sort of inner happiness more precious than anything we knew before finding the comfort of prayer.

CECIL (DE BLAGUIERE) HOWARD, *sculptor, served in the Office of Strategic Services during World War II. His works of sculpture include war memorials in France and others in the art museums of France, Eng-*

75

land, and the United States. He was awarded two gold medals for work shown in the Paris Exhibition of 1937; and the George Widener Gold Medal at Philadelphia in 1941. Mr. Howard is a past-president of the National Sculpture Society, and a member of the National Institute of Arts and Letters. He resides in New York.

DOROTHY B. HUGHES

I Say Good-Morning to God

As LONG as I can remember, prayer has been as much a part of the everyday as eating or sleeping or just breathing for me. It isn't necessary to make an on the knees production of prayer. It isn't even necessary to take time out from the day's routine. You can pray while you're at an office desk or feeding the baby, while you're driving your car or riding the subway, while you're waiting for your favorite TV program or while standing in line at a theatre. Talking to God is prayer. And because He is of the spirit, you speak to Him with your spirit, or, if you prefer, your mind or your inner heart. You don't need high-flown words to talk to Him, the simplest words are always the best.

On waking, to say good-morning to God, to offer Him everything I may do that day, gives a meaning and purpose to the day. It is prayer to speak to Him frequently during the day, even if to say no more than, "Thank you, Lord," for a pleasant moment, or to ask, "Help me, God," when the innumerable pinpricks arise. I wish it were possible to convey to those who do not go with God through their days, what a comfort it is not to walk alone but always with a friend.

I not only pity but I do not quite understand the man who, if he prays at all, uses prayer only as a demand in time of great stress or as an ejaculation at a time of unprecedented good fortune. I pity him because of his helplessness, because, whether or not he knows it, and certainly more than once he suspects it, he is a lost child wandering through the world's frightening darkness. I don't understand him because I fail to see how he can believe that he can carry the heavy burdens of this world alone. To be able to say and mean, "I put everything into your hands, Lord. Thy will be done," is the only hope of happiness in this life.

It seems to me that for modern survival we must return to the simple faith of our founding fathers, using prayer not as something special but as a part of the everyday. Not reserving God for the extraordinary events, but asking His blessing, simply, on our daily bread, knowing that if this be blessed, all else will be.

DOROTHY B. HUGHES, *author of many widely successful books, continues her literary work in California. She is a member of the Screen Writers' Guild.*

Prayer Is a Positive Force

Prayer is something that I do not reserve for moments of need. My father used to say that by communication with God through prayer the grace of being able to reach up and touch love comes to human beings. When I was a little boy I thought he meant I could stretch up and feel something with my fingers. Now that I am a man grown I know the meaning of what he was saying.

From prayer we derive comfort for our fears and sorrows, courage to go on. Prayer helps us make our choices, brings us out of negative into positive think-ing and feeling, for love is a positive force and prayer is our participation in the love we must have for each other that gives us self respect and respect for our fellows.

BURL IVES, *America's troubador, has been singing and traveling since his undergraduate days in the Twenties. He is the author of* Wayfaring Stranger *and other books.*

Faith

THE SIMPLE word "faith" sums up what I am convinced makes the difference between attaining or not attaining the greatest values of life.

The fully rounded faith has three interwoven parts:

1. Faith in yourself and your highest aspirations, which releases your creative inner powers and gives your daily life direction, adventure and meaning. 2. Faith in your fellow men, whom you love and serve. 3. Faith in God that answers the questions and longings of your soul—gives you help from the Higher Source—and sees the workings of the Creator in everything.

Faith can be a tremendous driving power throughout your practical daily living.

When you believe deeply that there is something worthwhile to do, you gain the spirit and energy to go out boldly in pursuit of new and greater goals.

It takes strength of character to *practice* religion. Yet the more it is used, the more it keeps forever building greater strength of character. It gives beliefs

80

you can hold fast to when everything else may seem to be crumbling. It is my conviction that faith is stronger than disbelief: faith can overcome fear and hopelessness in you, just as the whole history of mankind has been lighted up by the faiths that have triumphed over the forces of darkness.

Won't you join me in a prayer for a *living* faith?

A *daily* prayer:

O God, help us find the spark of soul
Thou hast dropped in every human being.
Help us live each day by faith—
Faith in our fellow men
    and in our highest aspirations;
Faith that brings us fellowship with Thee
And gives us eyes to see
God in everything.

Amen.

HENRY J. KAISER, *industrialist, has been called by Dr. Norman Vincent Peale "the greatest Builder of modern times." Dr. Peale asserts that Mr. Kaiser has not only had a major part in the building of three of the mightiest dams in the world—Hoover, Grand Coulee,* and Bonneville—and has built, in war-time, ships more rapidly and in greater number than was believed possible, but has also created enterprises in twenty-five different industries. "By his intense work," says Dr. Peale, "he proves that genius is perspiration as well as inspiration . . . His career is living proof of the miracle-working power of faith and a personal philosophy of the good life."

Prayer Fortifies and Strengthens

FROM my own experience I can say that prayer is a spiritual armor that fortifies and strengthens one in times of discouragement, trouble or sorrow.

Man must continually rededicate himself to God. Both silent and vocal prayer fortifies one's faith and strengthens one to meet emergencies of life with courage and without fear.

A famous scientist has said, "The most powerful form of energy one can create is prayer. Prayer, like radium, is a luminous and self-generating force of energy."

Today, in this third crisis to humanity in the last half century, we need a great faith—an adequate faith born in a rediscovery of our American heritage which lies rooted in religion, morality and democracy. In these days of gloom and doubt we must rededicate ourselves to the faith of our fathers. For our way of life to survive physically, it must be redeemed spiritually. God has answered the prayers of America in the past. Let us have faith that our prayers will also be heard today.

What can prayer do for us? It can give us new heart, a firmer spirit and a nobler attitude toward life. Like a divine prescription, prayer may be the one medicine that may cure our sick and stricken world. There is no substitute for prayer.

FRANK J. LAUSCHE, *Governor of the State of Ohio, began his fifth successive term in 1955, the only man ever five times Governor of that State in its entire 152-year history.*

EMMET LAVERY

Reach Out for the Life Force

WHEN MANY people pray together . . . they are in touch not only with each other but with a world more real than the one they can touch and see. They are reaching out for the very life force of the universe itself.

Pray then, I beg you, pray with a full heart and a full mind. Look deep into your souls—throw yourself upon the common will of God. . . .

And let us remember, my children, the lesson we have learned so often from the wise men of Greece . . . "There is nothing to fear in God. There is no pain in death. Good may be had, and the evil day *can* be endured" . . . good-night, my dear children, and may God's blessing be with you always.

EMMET LAVERY, *author of* Magnificent Yankee *and other stage and screen plays, has chosen these words as expressing his own thoughts on prayer. They are spoken by the Reverend Mother in the play,* Murder in a Nunnery, *which he dramatized from the novel by Eric Shepherd. Mr. Lavery is a member of the Screen Writers' Guild of Hollywood.*

My Silent Prayer

PRAYER has had a powerful influence in my life. I firmly believe in it and could speak at length on its effects just in my own life.

I think that the humility and confidence of an individual in his God, as expressed by prayer, undoubtedly wins His consideration and help. I have also found that if a person wants something, prayer also strengthens his will power and the goal is ultimately reached.

I am convinced that my silent prayer each day to make me a better servant of the people and to direct my efforts to the end that I will be a good Governor, makes it possible for me to meet all the problems and use better judgment. No man is sufficient unto himself; he needs the help of God.

J. BRACKEN LEE, *elected Governor of Utah in 1948, was re-elected in 1952 for the four-year term concluding in 1957.*

The Light that Guides Through All Darkness

Late one night a few weeks ago Mrs. Leonard and I left New York. The big plane lifted above the lights of the city then turned into utter darkness, guided by small flickering lights ten miles apart and 20,000 feet below. Then came the storm; and the clouds wiped out the lights. The storm grew worse, we went north many miles off our regular course. Several hours later the morning came and we recognized Lake Tahoe, Sacramento, the Bay Bridge. Through the storm there was a constant beam which guided that ship with sixty lives through an otherwise wilderness of blackness. In the plane was an instrument that was constantly tuned to that beam. No one could see it, but the pilot knew it was there.

In our confusion today we want to change the world—bring light, drive away storms, run from difficulty, grow despondent. But when our plane struck a strong wind, its engine bit deeper; when clouds came, it climbed higher above them; and when the small flickering lights on earth were hidden, it seized hold tightly of that unseen beam until full daylight came again. The plane could not change the weather, but it could overcome it. It had inner resources of beam and compass to which it was attuned.

I am not concerned that I cannot prove all that I believe. We cannot live only by what we can see. I have no proof of all that my religion holds. For I know that it is not with my eyes that I follow a beam, but with my spirit and with a faith that no storm is great enough to destroy it. I know from experience that when that spirit is tuned with that invisible power there is confidence, serenity, faith in myself and others, security and peace. I cannot change the world except as I change my power to live in it. Then my world, the only world I know, is changed.

If I had sufficient wealth to give each of you all that your heart desired, I could give you nothing of such value as the gift you can get for yourself by seizing hold of the beam that rose from Bethlehem. Let no man break your faith in that invisible light that guides our lives. It is real and it lives in the hearts of men everywhere. Remove it and men grow desperate beyond repair. There is not enough knowledge in the world to replace it.

Truly He said "If I be lifted up I will draw all men unto me." I am glad I can't see Him, for if I could my head would get ahead of my heart and spirit and

I would try by reason to prove Him false or true. But beyond my reach, I can get above my weakness, and through faith grow stronger as I reach for what I cannot comprehend. When we do this there is truly peace, and when men do it everywhere there is peace on earth and good will among men.

Prayer is the tie between the individual and the Great Spirit. It is the human soul searching for his relationship. Men cannot live greatly without it.

J. PAUL LEONARD *is president of San Francisco State College, at San Francisco, California.*

My Attitude Toward Prayer

THE MARINER is a devout man. He knows from his navigation that the stars are exact and that the constellations do not move by chance but according to the natural law. So complex are the signs he reads in the heavens and on the sea that he has no doubt of the Almighty Creator's Hand.

The power of prayer is one I am glad to acknowledge in my own life and the importance of the prayer-habit. Men have prayed in battle, in shipwreck, in storm, on a life-raft; men have prayed in temptation, in loneliness, in fear and in despair; men have prayed in bewilderment, in anxiety, in helplessness and in pity; men have prayed in defeat and in victory; men have prayed in happiness and in gratitude. Certainly our prayers have been answered and our hearts and hands strengthened, our lives enriched, our understanding deepened.

Men need to pray not only for themselves but for their friends, for their plans and for their country. Only by communication with their Creator can they place themselves at his service and only in his service is perfect freedom.

That is why at the U. S. Merchant Marine Academy religious services are well attended, every meal is preceded by a prayer for Grace, every graduation is opened and closed by prayer, and we kneel when we sing:

> Eternal Father, strong to save
> Whose arm doth bind the restless wave
> O hear us when we cry to Thee
> For those in peril on the sea.

I believe in prayer and in its efficacy. No habit is better for one's peace of mind than the submission of one's will to the Eternal Good and the nightly re-dedication of one's talents to the Creator's service. Thus obstacles are overcome and thus evil is defeated, and thus man steers toward that happy port which sailors call Haven. "So He bringeth them into their desired Haven." (Psalm 107, Verse 30.)

It goes without saying that prayer should be un-ostentatious, simple and from the heart or else it is not true prayer. We should remember Christ's injunction "But thou, when thou prayest, enter into thy closet, and when thou hast shut thy door, pray to thy Father which seeth in secret, and thy Father which seeth in secret shall reward thee openly." (Matt. 6:6)

And also "And all things, whatsoever ye shall ask in prayer, believing, ye shall receive." (Matt. 21:22)

In prayer it is the sincerity that counts.

REAR-ADMIRAL GORDON McLINTOCK, *born in Scotland and educated in England has served in the United States Maritime Commission, the Merchant Service, the Standard Oil Company and, during the Second World War, the United States Naval Reserve. Since 1948 he has been superintendent of the U. S. Merchant Marine Academy at Kings Point, Long Island.*

GEORGE CATLETT MARSHALL

A Soldier's Prayer

ALMIGHTY GOD:
May those who have given their lives in the service of this nation rest in Thy care.

May those who are wounded in body find spiritual comfort under Thy guidance in the knowledge that through their services a great cause has been served.

May those who offer their lives in support of that cause, by land, and sea, and air, find strength in Thy divine guidance.

May those of us who serve this nation in its great purpose to secure freedom for all peoples be sustained by Thy blessings.

Give us strength, O Lord, that we may be pure in heart and in purpose to the end that there may be peace on earth and good will among men.

May we be mindful this Easter morning "still stands Thine ancient sacrifice, an humble and a contrite heart."

Amen.

GEORGE CATLETT MARSHALL *served as Chief of Staff, United States Army during the Second World War, Secretary of State from 1947 to 1949, and Secretary of Defense from 1950 to 1951. In 1953, he was awarded the Nobel Peace Prize for his work with the United Nations. He spoke this prayer at the Sunrise Services held at the National Cemetery in Arlington, Virginia on Easter Morning, April 9, 1944, shortly before the collapse of Hitler's armies in World War II.*

Prayer Brings Its Own Answer

I CANNOT mention any outward or what might be considered any more "miraculous" answer to one prayer than to another. But, to me, the act of prayer brings its own answer in the calm and comfort to bear and endure that which may have seemed unbearable and unendurable.

MARY L. MASON *is the wife of the late Daniel Gregory Mason, musician and composer whose music lives in many hearts.*

MARIANNE MOORE

I Believe in Prayer

Yes, I BELIEVE in prayer—as a mystery which can endow one with more power perhaps than any other spiritual mystery, yet a mystery which cannot be exposited to the point where it is not a mystery. That Alexis Carrell's, Glenn Clark's, Richard C. Cabot's and others' statements about prayer, are applicably potent, and real, certainly is not a contradiction of what I have just said.

As when the apostle Peter objected, "Lord, depart from me for I am a sinful man," the paradox of faithful distrust, surely leads one to an apprehension of "faith." With regard to the efficacy of prayer "in communicating new courage" to the detached observer, however, courage to be derived from prayer will only be derived by those who make a trial of it.

MARIANNE CRAIG MOORE, *poet, was born in St. Louis and received her preparatory education in Carlisle, Pennsylvania, attended Bryn Mawr College briefly, and has since received honorary degrees from four colleges and universities. Three of her earliest pub-*

lished poems appeared in Contemporary Verse, in January, 1916. Her first volume, Poems was published in 1921. She received the Dial Award in 1924. Five other volumes of poetry followed before her Collected Poems was published in 1951. Her translation, in verse, of the Fables of La Fontaine, was published in 1954. Critical acclaim has brought her work, since the Dial Award, many awards including the National Institute of Arts and Letters Award, the Bollingen Prize in Poetry, the National Book Award, and the Pulitzer Prize for Poetry. Miss Moore resides in Brooklyn. She is a member of the National Institute of Arts and Letters.

Have Faith In God

IF I COULD relive my days I would effect a sizable shift of emphasis. I believe that I placed too much emphasis on learning how to make a living and not enough in learning how to live.

I can see now that I should have grasped the opportunity to learn something about the transcendent importance of religion and liberty and morality in the lives of all people, everywhere.

We engineers are taught to adapt the forces of nature to the uses of man. But I failed to grasp the significance of the most vital force of all—the spiritual strength of the individual being.

I have no one to blame for this but myself. *The knowledge was there for the taking.*

For I have observed that in those places where the people have brought into their daily living the principles of God's moral code—in those places there is liberty and morality and charity, and there the people have become rich in life's blessings.

I use morality and charity in the broadest sense. By morality I mean individual responsibility for one's honorable conduct. And by charity I mean Judean-Christian concern for one's neighbor.

I have known many men in many different kinds of activity. And I have concluded that in every field of human endeavor the application of the moral code, or our failure to apply it, has vitally affected our social, political and economic conduct and, ultimately, our national well-being and our national security.

I believe that any effort to draw a line of demarcation between moral teachings and secular teachings is not only ill-advised; it is futile. The effects of our actions, conscious and unconscious, in every field, whether it be diplomacy, or making steel or playing a game of football, are dependent upon our understanding of the moral code and the degree to which we permit it to influence our decisions.

Now you may ask—Why does a representative of American industry attach such great importance to this matter of spiritual strength? It is because I believe that it is the source of that power which is essential for our ultimate victory.

We have been able to produce so abundantly because here in America we have had individual liberty, which is in conformity with the basic tenets of our faith. We have had freedom for the individual to be secure in his life, his liberty and his possessions, to save and to venture, to risk and to gain and to be responsible for the results of his own decisions and his own actions for better or for worse.

Here in this country we have carried into our daily living the precepts of the moral code which alone has permitted us *to have individual liberty.*

Without morality, liberty becomes license—to deprive others of their rights and liberties and to avoid responsibility for one's actions and for one's neighbors in need. Without charity, morality is a selfish thing without reason or purpose.

I believe this is the meaning of St. Paul's message to the Corinthians, "Where the spirit of the Lord is, there is liberty."

It seems to me that if we have faith in God, we must realize that He had a purpose in designing us so that no person is like any other person; that is to say, so that each person is an individual.

It must be obvious that liberty necessarily means freedom to choose foolishly as well as wisely; freedom to choose evil as well as good; freedom to enjoy the rewards of good judgment, and freedom to suffer the penalties of bad judgment. If this is not true, the word "freedom" has no meaning.

It is important to note that every society which has belittled the importance of the individual and has attempted to treat humanity in the mass has also

100

eventually belittled religious teachings and faith amongst its people. To me this is an inevitable sequence. The spirit of God does not reside in a group of people as such. The teachings of Christ invariably deal with the status of the individual. It is only the individual who can feel and live by religious faith.

I propose that each one of us should renew his devotion to those things which we hold sacred; that we pray to the source of all strength for strength and courage to do our solemn duty; that with understanding of each other and with humility in the sight of God we resolve to hold fast in the face of any and all discouragements. With this spirit we will win through!

BEN MOREELL, *Admiral, United States Navy, and chairman of the board, Jones & Laughlin Steel Company since 1952, was born in Salt Lake City, Utah, in 1892 and was graduated from St. Louis University in 1913. Appointed to the Civil Engineers Corps, U. S. Navy, in 1917, he advanced through the grades to the rank of Admiral in 1936. He was chief of civil engineers from 1937 to 1945, retiring in 1946. Admiral Moreell is a past president of the American Society of Military Engineers and is the author of several books on engineering. He resides in Pittsburgh.*

The Value of Prayer to Me

WHEN Abraham Lincoln left his home town of Springfield, Illinois, for Washington, to become President of the United States, he asked but one thing of those old and tried Springfield friends who went to the station to see him off: "Pray for me."

Lincoln served his country during one of the darkest periods of history. During those trying times, he valued the fact that others prayed for him and for the nation. He, himself, prayed . . . with an intensity and sincerity that impressed historians.

Thus prayer meant much to Abraham Lincoln . . . and to this great country of ours in a time of crisis.

Repeatedly, the power of prayer has been demonstrated by incidents in the lives of our great leaders. It also has been demonstrated in the every day experiences of men and women in all walks of life . . . men and women who have found peace through a trust and faith in God.

Prayer is often misused. We frequently forget that when Christ taught us to pray, He used these words, "Thy will be done. . . ."

Too often we selfishly pray for personal things . . . and then are bitter when our prayers aren't answered. Would it have been completely fair to others for our prayers to have been answered?

Our prayers should be personal, but they should not be selfish. They should always be that "Thy will be done. . . ." They should be made in a spirit of thankfulness for the blessings that have already been ours . . . for Christ who died on the cross for us. They should be made humbly.

Perhaps the most we should ask of God when we pray is for His help in living our lives in such a way that we will deserve the best He has to offer.

As we pray for others, forgetting our own selfish wants, there comes that inner peace and good feeling that mark the truly successful person.

And our prayers should be accompanied by faith.

The story is told of a woman who had to climb a high hill each day to get from her little home to the well from which she obtained her water supply. One day after a number of tiring trips to the well, the woman decided that what she should do was pray to God to remove that hill.

Worn out from the day's trips across the hill, the woman prayed that night before she put her tired body into her little bed.

She awakened the next day, rushed to the window

and looked out. The hill was still there, presenting just as much of an obstacle as ever.

The woman said: "It's just like I thought. I knew it would still be there."

She had prayed . . . but without faith.

Today our nation and our world are in a very grave condition. Never was there a time—and our country has faced many a crisis—when universal prayer was more badly needed. Prayer is powerful.

If each of us would pause to offer a prayer to God in our own words, or even silently, that peace come, perhaps that would accomplish what treaties, discussions —even fighting—have been unable to bring about.

Perhaps our prayers for peace would be answered through some of the organizations and methods already set up, but peace would come, if we prayed intently, unselfishly, sincerely, humbly and with faith.

Just as Lincoln prayed as he began his second term as President, our prayer today might well be ". . . to do all which may achieve and cherish a just and lasting peace . . . with all nations."

JOHNSTON MURRAY *was Governor of Oklahoma, 1950-1954.*

104

Script, Before Final Draft

I HAVE been deep in a script. I start the final redraft tomorrow. Will prayer help me?

I do not know. I am still too confused and wondering a fellow to have found any clear religious direction yet—too lost in nineteenth century scientific materialism, that bog of the human soul—to have yet arrived at any formal and organized faith. I am sure I am a Christian, but, for me, dogma still stands in the way of creed; and, to me, prayer is not at all what the orthodox mean by the word, but merely *a way of thinking by myself,* and a mystical belief in the incarnation of the Holy Spirit in all men. . . .

I am for all sincere faiths that worship the invisible God, under whatever name, and love men as His highest manifestation, and tolerate the religious divagations of others. I am sure it is one of the finest and most helpful things in the experience of Man, if it rises from the heart to the lips, as water from a well; but not everyone has learned to use the pump; and some insist—wrongly, I think—that it must always be a standardized make of pump. I am equally sure that if the world ever follows the way of the Jesus of the Four Gospels all our troubles will be over. That way seems intolerably hard, perhaps, and Man may never try it till he has brought his world to ashes. . . .

I have been deep in a script. I start the final redraft tomorrow.

DUDLEY NICHOLS, *in World War I an American naval officer on hazardous duty in the North Sea, next a newspaperman, and now, as he has been for thirty years, a writer of successful scripts for Hollywood, is the author of such screen plays as* The Informer *(which won the Academy Award) and* The Bells of St. Mary's, *which was honored in 1954 by the Screen Writers' Guild with its highest award— the Laurel Achievement.*

J. HOWARD PEW

Enlist Under God

BEFORE we attempt to lead other nations toward peace, we first must reaffirm our own faith in the moral and spiritual principles of Christianity, so that we shall be strong enough to resist the invasion of Communism and other alien influences. Individually and nationally, we must cleanse our minds of all dishonest thinking. We must strive constantly for honesty in government, in politics, in business, and in our private lives. We must rededicate ourselves to the service of God, and be ready at all times to give a "reason for the faith that is in us."

Which road is the world to take? The road to Christianity or the road to paganism? There is no other. Here in America, during the last 100 years, the Christian road has provided the world with the greatest spectacle of human progress ever witnessed throughout history. It was achieved only because there was complete religious freedom and a wide-open invitation to all the genius, inventive ability, organizing capacity, and managerial skill of a great people.

It is Christianity that has brought us to this high

estate; and out of Christianity has flowed religious freedom, intellectual freedom, political freedom— freedom to dream, to think, to experiment, to invent, to match wits in friendly competition; freedom to be an individual. That is our great Christian heritage.

To each of us is assigned a part to play in the great drama of life; and we can only play our parts with the greatest measure of perfection as free, Christian individuals.

Let us resolve, as did Abraham Lincoln four score and seven years ago, "that this nation, under God, shall have a new birth of freedom—and that government of the people, by the people, for the people, shall not perish from the earth."

J. Howard Pew, *industrialist, entered the oil refining industry in 1901 and became president of the Marcus Hook Refinery eleven years later, remaining its president to 1947. He is now a director of the Sun Shipbuilding & Dry Dock Company. His home, "Knollbrook," is at Ardmore, Pennsylvania.*

On Prayer

For many years prayer has been an inconspicuous feature of my daily routine. I suppose I allot to it about the same amount of time at night as I do to setting up exercises in the morning. The daily prayer has usually been the same prayer, a stereotyped form of words, often run through while my mind has been wandering. There have been periods, as during the Second World War, when I prayed every day with real fervor. My son was overseas for nearly four years. At other times, the critical illness of persons dear to me has caused me to pray with special earnestness. Although I gave thanks, I was not able to attribute to my prayers the safe return of my son or the recovery of my sick friends. Too many young men did not return whose fathers, very likely more worthy than I, prayed for them just as earnestly. Sick people are dying every day notwithstanding the prayers of those who hold them dear. It would indeed be presumptuous for me to ascribe the return of my son and the recovery of any sick friends to the divine intervention that I had invoked. I cannot believe that God is

109

a respecter of persons, or that arbitrarily, for reasons beyond human comprehension, He grants one man's prayer and denies that of his neighbor.

Is there a difference when prayer concerns itself not with personal and relatively selfish interests, but with great causes which embody the highest aspirations of humanity? World peace, the brotherhood of man, the triumph of the United Nations over bellicose nationalism and aggressive Communism—have not all of us who are given to the habit of prayer concentrated with some earnestness on such themes during the last six months? We shall continue so to concentrate, even though there is no evidence as yet to suggest that our efforts are destined to receive a clearly favorable and definitive response.

Leaving aside the question of the definite answer to the specific prayer, I do not doubt the value of prayer. In situations of intense seriousness, to pray is often all that one can do. When one has done all that one can, there is release from tension; the mind begins to operate again in a normal and useful manner. The principal value of prayer lies not in what it brings to the person or nation or cause that is its theme, but in its effect on the mental attitude of him who prays.

I have heard many sermons preached on prayer. It is probably owing to my unfortunate skepticism, which I should like to discard but cannot, that most of them left me unmoved and unconvinced. In one sentence, it seems to me, George Meredith set forth the function of prayer and what it may accomplish. "Who rises from prayer a better man, his prayer is answered." I would not venture to affirm that the daily habit of many years, followed too often perfunctorily, has produced any significant improvement in a character full of flaws. Yet the hope exists and is a strengthening influence.

ARTHUR STANWOOD PIER, *long distinguished as an educator and writer, is a member of the National Institute of Arts and Letters.*

Success Through God's Help

I HAVE never for a minute believed that any success of mine could have been attained without God's help, nor have I ever embarked on any undertaking without asking His help. I would feel very lonely indeed if I didn't know He was within the sound of my voice.

RONALD REAGAN, *born in Illinois, began his career as a motion picture actor in 1937. He served as a captain in the United States Air Force in World War II. He is a past president of the Screen Actors' Guild.*

Pray for, and Protect, Peace

CREATIVE minds, in searching, have at last stum-
bled upon omnipotence! For centuries creative
intelligence has eagerly given all to end war and then
failed utterly to protect the peace.

With the atomic bomb and our other secrets, if we
act quickly, we shall witness the colossal collapse of
ego and of error—the climax and culmination of centuries of slaughter and destruction—the summation
and end forever of man's inhumanity to man.

In the Great Tomorrow the merit system, that now
governs the athlete, shall guarantee to all men an open
road and a fair chance, under strict rules, enforced by
wise and impeccable referees. Men and nations shall
be exalted for what they create—for what they give
to the world, not for what they squander and destroy.
In the Great Tomorrow men shall learn that to *give*
abundantly is the only way to *reap* abundantly. The
super-man of Tomorrow's history shall be he who is
the servant of all.

R. S. REYNOLDS *is chairman of the board of the Reynolds Metal Company, Richmond, Virginia.*

Prayer Is the Bread of Life

PRAYER, to me, is the bread of Life, and without it we eventually starve spiritually. The hope of our country is help from God to fill men with His Holy Spirit so they may learn to "Love Thy Neighbor as Thyself"—and this can only be obtained through constant prayer.

DALE EVANS ROGERS, *wife of Roy Rogers, is author of the best-selling book,* Angel Unaware.

114

Pray Every Day

I AM PROUD to say that I pray every day. Our Forefathers, who founded this country, prayed—and if we want to keep our wonderful country free from the darkness that threatens us, we'd better all pray—and pray hard.

ROY ROGERS, *born in Cincinnati in 1912, was starred in his first movie,* Under Western Skies, *in 1938. He has since starred in seventy-five western pictures, in most of which he rode his famous horse,* Trigger. *He is a member of the Screen Actors' Guild and other associations.*

The Good Life

WHEN I was quite young I heard and learned of many different attitudes toward prayer. My maternal grandmother and grandfather were very orthodox people, and very early I knew of and obeyed the orthodox tenets of the Jewish religion. My paternal grandfather was not nearly as orthodox, and as a matter of fact was quite irreligious. My mother and father kept an orthodox Jewish home mainly out of respect to their parents and to the Jewish community in which they lived, which generally was orthodox, but I learned that both my mother and father did not believe deeply in certain things, such as dietary laws, even though they observed them religiously because of their background and because of the catering business which they maintained on a strictly kosher basis.

This wide divergence of religious attitude was not confusing to me. However, it did make me search for some answer of my own and for an individual point of view. While still young I learned that God would not punish you if you ate bread during Passover, nor would He punish you for other slight infractions.

These naive observations seemed quite important to me when I was fourteen, and certainly were in direct opposition to my grandfather's strict patriarchal point of view.

It was my grandmother who taught me my early Hebrew evening prayers. She made them of particular significance to me when I was Bar Mitzvahed at thir-teen. Her warm attitude about this prayer and her explanation of it made me view it as an affirmation of faith. When I discussed it with my mother, she gave it a further luminance for me, and for the first time I considered prayer without fear—and in the years since, my convictions about prayer have become strengthened particularly as I regard the world in which we live.

Too often I have met religious peoples of all faiths who are not actually and deeply conscious either of their religious heritage or history. On the other hand, I have met "irreligious" people who are truly and deeply religious, in that they live with basic and deep affection for all men. I do not make the point that all orthodox or religious people are bad or that all "irreli-gious" people are good. I am merely making the point that the practice of religious dogma does not make a man religious. Further, I believe that all people who pray do not necessarily pray for the best things. With perhaps an iconoclastic point of view, I believe that a man best lives his religion by practicing it in terms of his relationship to his fellow man and less in terms of his prayer book.

In our Talmud we are told that a good Jew is that man who lives the good life in God's way toward his fellow man, and we are further told that God forgives that man who lives the good life and who may even forget his daily prayer.

But I happen to feel deeply about prayer and about daily prayer—particularly if that prayer is pronounced in love and affection and less in fear—particularly if the prayer is broad and general in scope and less selfish—particularly if the things prayed for are for the enrichment of the soul and mind, and less for the material comforts or gains—particularly if the *mea culpas* in all religions are beaten less on the chest and more often in the heart and mind.

Too often prayer to me is used for sacrilegious purposes. God is not an employment agency and cannot get us a good job if we are out of work. God is not a dramatic critic, and cannot get us good notices for a bad play. God is not a hoodlum for hire, who will strike down our enemies for us. God is not a farm hand, who will till those forty acres.

Prayer should combine a pledge of faith plus an

examination of one's own motives and purposes. Prayer, as it affirms our faith and love of God, should plead for a continuance or for a restoration of our humility and courage and decency and dignity and judgment and wisdom. With these prayers we will find a strengthening of these general characteristics within ourselves, and if we practice these virtues we will find them in our fellow man—and in doing that we will be doing God's work here on earth.

People who are strained and tired and confused will find that prayer will act as a catharsis that rids them of their weariness and strain and confusion. As they pray for peace of mind through self-examination, they will be blessed with an ease and comfort of spirit that will bring them comfort and objectivity.

The trouble with most people who say they don't believe in anything is that they don't work hard enough at trying to believe.

A strong man cannot be strong unless he exercises his muscles.

A wise man cannot be wise unless he exercises wisdom.

Good!

A man with faith in God cannot keep that faith unless he exercises it.

That is why I believe in prayer.

DORE SCHARY, *motion picture producer and writer, author of thirty-five screen plays, has been executive vice-president of Metro-Goldwyn-Mayer in charge of production and studio operations since 1948. His production of* The Story of Boys' Town *brought him the Academy Award in 1948 for the best picture of the year. He also produced, in addition to screen plays of his own authorship, sixteen other notably successful pictures. Born in Newark, New Jersey, in 1905, he has resided in California since 1932.*

True Prayer Takes Many Forms

I HAVE heard it said that prayer is a private, personal matter, confined to such moments when the individual isolates himself from the external world and speaks out of his heart and soul to his God. To the extent that it is his means of spiritual communication, whether he kneels by his bed at night or whispers a prayer in his heart in the midst of a busy day in town, that is true.

But I think most of us sooner or later recognize that prayer is also a public matter, a community affair, a means of publicly attesting our faith in God. The churches, the public gatherings for the purpose of praying in time of crisis or doubt, are obvious examples of this fact. Yet it is also important to realize that prayer interpenetrates, so to speak, our daily business lives—publicly or openly.

The best example of this that comes to mind is the National Conference of Christians and Jews. Here in this organization we see prominent men of widely differing faiths, often rivals in business, getting together publicly to promote tolerance and spirituality in our daily lives. To me, their very presence at these meetings or even banquets is one of the noblest examples of man's urge to reveal his reliance upon God's will.

Watching business men at these functions it has occurred to me, more than once, that even their casual act of clapping their hands to applaud a speaker is actually, if incongruously, a form of prayer.

J. WATERS SCHWAB, *president of J. R. Wood and Sons, Inc., of New York City, is Chairman of the Jewelry Industry Committee of the National Conference of Christians and Jews.*

Nothing Has Meant More to Me

MAN IN EVERY age and in every land has believed in the power and the efficacy of prayer. This belief has been based upon the consciousness of human limitations and an instinctive faith in the existence of some Being more powerful in the universe. It is natural, therefore, for men to pray. And all men do somehow and at some times cry out to something beyond themselves for help.

Prayers have been offered to all sorts of things; animals, idols, natural objects, and the like. Strange and unusual modes of prayer have been developed, and complicated rituals of prayer have been devised. But back of them all lies the universal need of an individual human being for communion with deity. The Christian religion, more perfectly than others, fulfills that need.

For our Lord and Savior Jesus Christ prayer was as simple and direct as conversation with an earthly parent. It required no special place, posture or language. It was an uninterrupted companionship with the Heavenly Father. He taught His disciples the most perfect of all prayers and set them an example of praying at all times and under all circumstances. No one who does not pray can be one of His followers. And Christians everywhere know and bear testimony to the comfort, guidance, and strength which prayer brings to them.

As a humble follower of the Lord Jesus, I gladly bear such testimony. In my own personal experience, nothing has meant more to me than the daily habit of prayer.

WILLIAM KERR SCOTT *served as Governor of North Carolina from 1948 to 1953. He has been president of the National Association of Commissioners of Agriculture and has also been interested in encouragement of the cotton and tobacco industries. He resides at Haw River, North Carolina.*

ADLAI E. STEVENSON

The Prayer of St. Francis of Assisi

THIS prayer by St. Francis of Assisi is my favorite prayer:

Lord make me an instrument of Thy peace; where there is hatred, let me sow love; where there is injury, pardon; where there is doubt, faith; where there is despair, hope; where there is darkness, light; and where there is sadness, joy.

O Divine Master, grant that I may not so much seek to be consoled as to console; to be understood, as to understand; to be loved, as to love; for it is in giving that we receive, it is in pardoning that we are pardoned, and it is in dying that we are born to eternal life.

ADLAI EWING STEVENSON *was the Democratic nominee for the Presidency of the United States in 1952.*

Why I Pray Daily

I BELIEVE that prayer helps me in two principal ways:

In the first place, it re-affirms my faith in God. Fruitful experience with prayer, through the years, has dispelled from my mind all doubt about the existence of an Infinite Being—a source of great strength with which to face and solve the problems of daily life. It has been said that religion is betting your life that there is a God. The stimulating and helpful experiences which have come to me through prayer have proved to me that God exists.

This Divine Power may, I think, (and I say it with all reverence) be likened to a radio station, which is constantly sending out waves in every direction. I know from experience that when I turn on my own receiving set and tune it properly, through prayer, I find God and God finds me. It is a fellowship very much like the relationship between partners. I am not impressed by the testimony of those who, never having turned on their own sets, assert that there is no God.

Secondly, the act of prayer affords me a splendid

opportunity for self-appraisal. It helps me to determine and then focus my thinking on the high objectives which, as one who believes in God, I aspire to attain. Thoreau once asked—

"Did you ever hear of a man who had striven all his life faithfully and singly toward an object and in no measure obtained it? If a man constantly aspires, is he not elevated?

"Did ever a man try heroism, magnanimity, truth, sincerity and find that there was no advantage in them—that it was a vain endeavor?"

In daily meditation and communion with God we gain a needed sense of true humility. That helps us to think about what God wants for us rather than in terms of what we want.

It is sobering to realize that we can never expect to find God in a mind soiled by base thoughts or by selfish motives. On the other hand, if we seek God daily in prayer and, in our prayers, set our mental sights in the direction of our highest ideals and aspirations we find God. Thus we gain inward peace and assurance; and experience limitless satisfactions and happiness.

Dr. William E. Stevenson *is president of Oberlin College, founded in 1833 in Oberlin, Ohio, the first co-educational college in the United States.*

GALE STORM

Strength Flowing From God

WHEN I pray I feel that I am reaching within myself to the strength and power that is constantly flowing from God through each individual. The more I pray, in the right way, the more boundless become my energies, and the more direction my life takes on in the furtherance of the Christian way of life.

GALE STORM, *radio actress, is known to millions of Americans through her radio roles.*

128

The Best Prayer Is: A Good Life

THERE is, deep in each of us, a sense of thanks-giving when things go well and we are in good health. That could be put into words and called prayer. And there is, with even greater force, a sense of supplication for protection when we feel fore-bodings and premonitions.

But the trouble with those of us who do not believe in an immediate and personal God lies in their in-ability to translate thoughts and feelings into words. Perhaps among some there is to be found a reluctance. Galsworthy put it this way:

> "O Lord of Courage grave,
> O Master of this night of Spring!
> Make firm in me a heart too brave
> To ask Thee anything."

Prayer undoubtedly is helpful, but sometimes it is used as a substitute for rectitude. Again I quote— this time from Coleridge:

> "He prayeth well who loveth well
> Both man and bird and beast.
> He prayeth best who loveth best

All things both great and small;
For the dear God who loveth us,
He made and loveth all."

Prayers are the expression of a relationship between us and God—call Him what you please and worship Him as you will. They are an admission of a higher power. They make for a humility and prove that no one of us is wholly self sufficient. They are the basis for us to hold "a decent respect for the opinions of mankind."

Prayers for self gain are not worthwhile. Prayers for the strengthening of faith—for the stimulation of the spiritual are uplifting and ennobling.

Do not make a prayer a beggar's appeal. Do not try to jog God's elbow to remind Him of what you may think is His duty. Avoid the danger of patting God upon the head.

A good life is the best prayer. And Peace is the thing most worth praying for.

HERBERT BAYARD SWOPE, *newspaperman and publicist, winner of the Pulitzer Prize in 1917 for his reports from Europe immediately preceding the entry of the United States into World War I, executive*

130

editor of the *New York* World, *in a brilliant decade of that newspaper's life, and recipient of the 1950 Gold Medal Award of the Interfaith-in-Action Committee for his "notable achievements in fostering interfaith and inter-racial understanding," has been a moving spirit in the work of Freedom House, since its foundation.*

What Is *Prayer?*

Is it not the most intense concentration of the mind and soul in an effort to penetrate beyond one's own limitations to a greater mind, a greater soul, to ultimate creative energy, and ultimate truth?

We close our eyes to pray in order to shut out the world we know and to concentrate on that for which we aspire.

The commonest, often unconscious prayer is "God Help Me!"

But help me *how,* and to what?

Do not our prayers for help mean: Help me to be better than I know myself to be. Help me to do this thing that I am doing better than my own limited capacities would permit without help. Help me to restrain my passions about to flare. Help me to discipline my tired mind. Help me to open my heart and imagination. Help me toward that wisdom which is more than knowledge. Help me to kindle and rekindle the divine spark of love. Help me to find the fortitude by which I may endure this sorrow, frustration, injustice, or disappointment. God help me to know, love, and trust in God and to perform his particular will for me?

Everyone who has ever tried to do or to endure something beyond his normal limitations reaches out to the force greater than himself, the Mind and Spirit that created Creation itself. And he often does so when he does not even know he is praying.

I have known creative artists who proclaimed themselves atheists. But beset with the tortures often attending the creative process they, too, turned to the super-creative force in a search which is, whatever one calls it, Prayer.

I seldom "say my prayers." But I pray—a dozen, a score, or more times a day, reaching out in every moment of intense concentration for help. Almost always it comes. If it does not, I know I have prayed in the wrong way or for the wrong things.

I know that without prayer I would live far below the level which, with the help of God, I can reach. I know that even with this help it is a level miserably low. But it would be base, but for strength and inspiration won through prayer.

For this strength and inspiration my heart sings in perpetual praise. Thus prayer, which begins with a cry, ends in a song of joy.

Dorothy Thompson, *internationally-known commentator on political affairs, in newspapers, magazines, on the radio and the lecture platform, is a member of the American Academy of Political and Social Sciences and an honorary member of Phi Beta Kappa. She is married and makes her home in New York City.*

Our Only Sure Foundation

I HAVE just come from the National Cemetery at Arlington, where I laid a wreath on the grave of an American hero. No American knows, no real American cares, whether that man was a Catholic, a Jew or a Protestant, or what his origin or color were. That grave—the Grave of the Unknown Soldier—symbolizes our faith in unity.

I am trying to get all those people who look up and who know that there is a greater power than man in the universe to organize themselves to meet those who look down and who are strictly materialistic.

It is only the people of religious faith throughout the world who have the power to overcome the force of tyranny. It is in their beliefs that the path can be found to justice and freedom. Their religious concepts are the only sure foundation of the demo-cratic ideal.

Sustained and strengthened by one another, we can go forward, under God, to meet and overcome the difficulties which confront us. With His help, mankind will come at last to a world where peace, freedom and justice will be enjoyed by all people everywhere.

HARRY S. TRUMAN, *thirty-third president of the United States, made this declaration in a speech before the National Conference of Christians and Jews on November 11, 1949, the thirty-first Anniversary of the Armistice ending the First World War.*

136

A *Prayer for Collegians*

THE PRAYER I enjoy using most is one first uttered by Peter Marshall, late Chaplain of the United States Senate. It represents a deep faith in our religion as well as our political way of life—a faith I hope to make real to the young men and women attending Rollins College.

"Oh God, our Father, we pray that the people of America, who have made such progress in material things, may now seek to grow in spiritual understanding.

"For we have improved means, but not improved ends. We have better ways of getting there, but we have no better places to go. We can save more time, but we are not making any better use of the time we save.

"We need Thy help to do something about the world's true problems. The problem of lying, which is called propaganda; the problem of selfishness, which is called self-interest; the problem of greed, which is often called profit; the problem of license, disguising itself as liberty; the problem of lust, masquerading as love; the problem of materialism, the hook which is baited with security.

"Hear our prayer, Oh, Lord, for the spiritual understanding which is better than political wisdom, that we may see our problems for what they are. This we ask in Jesus' name. Amen."

PAUL A. WAGNER, *president of Rollins College, Winter Park, Florida, was called to that post in 1950 at the age of 33.*

A Keeper in Whom I Put My Trust

GOD TO ME is a very nebulous concept. I cannot conceive that such a being exists or that I have a right, if He does, to intrude on Him with my micro-scopic affairs.

At the same time, I cannot exclude myself from a total world consciousness which is beyond my com-prehension. The imagination is its keeper, in whom I put my trust.

WILLIAM CARLOS WILLIAMS, *poet, born September 17, 1883, entered the practice of medicine—in which he still continues—after his graduation from the University of Pennsylvania in 1906 and a further year of study at the University of Leipzig, Germany. His* Selected Poems *were published in 1949, his* Auto-biography *in 1951. Dr. Williams was awarded the*

Dial Prize "for service to American literature" in 1926; the National Book Award in poetry, 1949; the Bollingen Prize in poetry, 1953. He is a member of the National Institute of Arts and Letters, and the recipient of honorary degrees from the universities of Buffalo, Rutgers, and Pennsylvania. Dr. Williams' home is in Rutherford, New Jersey, his birthplace.

Why We Pray

Life for all of us at times seems to be unreasonably harsh or even cruel—a field of wheat is destroyed by hail the day before the farmer was going to harvest it, a home burns, a man with a family loses his job, a strike throws thousands out of work, a small child is stricken by polio, a little boy has his throat cut by a fiend, a mother dies in childbirth, an only son is lost in Korea, a fine capable man is stricken by a heart attack before his time. Certainly it is a sound religious and social objective to protect men and women to the degree possible against the hazards of life, but this cannot be done by destroying individual responsibility or depriving the millions of their freedom.

I am sure that it is the very nature of man to aspire to be free. The spirit of man requires freedom just as a plant requires sunshine. Therefore the people of a nation cannot be happy, prosperous and contented under any form of society which represses them as individuals and limits their personal freedom in both a spiritual and material sense. The best definition I have heard of freedom is one Cardinal Mooney gave me:

"Freedom is the condition under which a person is not restrained in the exercise of any right or the fulfilment of any responsibility."

This desire of man to be free is consistent with the ethical and religious principles taught in our churches, and we will certainly make more progress as human beings in a free society than we could under any form of tyranny. It is doubtful if a free society can continue to exist unless the great majority of the people have religious beliefs and subscribe to a body of ethical principles. This is why those who want to undermine a free society attack the churches. Religious leaders are the first to suffer when the people lose their liberty. I am also sure that a free people will make the most progress in raising their standard of living, improving their health and contributing to their spiritual happiness.

In speaking of tolerance and especially of religious tolerance, I would like to make the sharp distinction between tolerance and indifference. I am sure that tolerance is essential to a free society, but I am even more convinced that no free society can continue to exist unless the great majority of its citizens have religious beliefs and subscribe to ethical principles and

142

a moral code that develops self-respect and self-discipline on the part of individuals and recognition of the individual citizen's basic obligations to others. With this background he will be willing to concede to others the same rights that he wishes to enjoy himself.

My special plea is that all of us should renew our confidence and faith in our type of free society and that all of us should work to further social and economic progress based on the common ethical principles of our religions and as expressed in the Constitution of our country.

CHARLES E. WILSON, *Secretary of Defense in the Cabinet of President Eisenhower, expressed these thoughts when president of General Motors Corporation.*